TAX FACTS 3

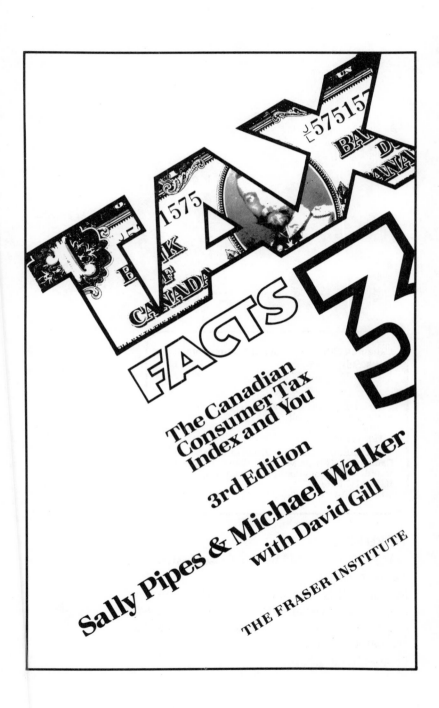

TAX FACTS 3

The Canadian Consumer Tax Index and You

3rd Edition

Sally Pipes & Michael Walker

with David Gill

THE FRASER INSTITUTE

Canadian Cataloguing in Publication Data
Pipes, Sally, 1945-
   Tax facts 3

   First ed. published 1976 under title: How
much tax do you really pay?
   Bibliography: p.
   ISBN 0-88975-044-0
   1. Taxation—Canada.   2. Tax incidence—
Canada.   I. Walker, Michael, 1945-   II. Gill,
David.   III. Fraser Institute (Vancouver,
B.C.)   IV. Title.
HJ2451.H69 1982   336.2'00971   C82-091087-2

THIRD EDITION.

Printed in Canada.

Contents

Tables and Figures

TABLES

FIGURES

Preface

This book is a summary of the latest results of a Fraser Institute project that began in July, 1975. The objective of the project was to find out how much tax, in all forms, Canadians pay to federal, provincial and municipal governments and how the size of this tax bill has changed from 1961 to the present. The study analyzes Canada's tax system in each of six years, 1961, 1969, 1972, 1974, 1976, and 1978. The years 1961 and 1969 were chosen because they have been the focus of major studies in the past. Neither of these major studies attempted to link their findings together over several years. The Fraser Institute study has done this and has incorporated the 1978 data, which are the latest released by Statistics Canada at the time of writing. In addition, we have also prepared estimates for 1980.

It will come as no surprise to anybody that we found the system of taxation to be very complicated and that its structure closely resembles that of an onion. The process of cutting through the layers of taxation also provided its share of tearful moments—both because of its difficulty and because of what we found. We are publishing this guide to taxation in Canada to make the results of our in-depth study accessible to taxpayers who are concerned about the tax explosion in recent years but who have neither the time nor the inclination to wade into the forbidding taxation jungle.

The book has been written with two distinct purposes in mind: first, to provide a non-technical do-it-yourself manual so that the average Canadian family can calculate how much tax they really pay; second, to update a statistic, first published in 1976, that we call the Canadian Consumer Tax Index. This index measures how much the tax bill of an average Canadian family has increased since 1961 and by how much it is changing currently. In other words, it measures changes in the price that Canadians pay for government.

This book does not attempt to look at the benefits that Canadians receive from government in return for their taxes. Rather, it looks at the price that is paid for a product —government. It has nothing to say about the quality of the product, how much of it each of us receives, or whether we get our money's worth. These questions, essential though they are, must be considered in another study. Evidently, the Institute reflected a general curiosity— perhaps anxiety—about the price we pay for government when it first published its work on taxation in 1976. *How Much Tax Do You Really Pay?* was judged to be a bestseller in Canada.

A defect of the earlier studies was the fact that they did not contain province-by-province data on the burden of taxation. Some readers indicated that they wanted to know their tax burden in their province of residence. They will now be able to compare their own tax burden with the burden which exists in other provinces.

A criticism levied at our previous study, *How Much Tax Do You Really Pay?* was that it ignored the extent to which governments finance their expenditures by issuing debt. As one observer remarked, "Governments can only finance their expenditures by taxing or printing money. When they issue bonds they are only deferring the process of taxation or delaying the printing of money. There is a limit on the extent they can do this and we should therefore peer through the veil of debt to the ultimate tax and money printing implications of government finance."[1] Accordingly, in this third edition, we have made explicit calculations of the tax burden including and excluding the current deficit position of governments at all levels.

The Fraser Institute calculations of tax burden are part of an on-going program of research. In making these results available to the public we seek both to inform and to be informed. Readers who disagree with our methods or conclusions are invited to write to the Institute to convey the nature of their reservations. In this way, our methods and our estimates can be refined and hopefully perfected.

We are pleased to acknowledge the assistance of Mrs. Gail Oja, Director, Consumer Income and Expenditure Division, Statistics Canada, who provided certain unpublished background data which were essential to the study. The Canadian Tax Simulator computer programs were written by David Gill whose unsparing efforts we are pleased to acknowledge.

Sally Pipes
Michael Walker

About the Authors

MICHAEL A. WALKER

Michael A. Walker is Director of The Fraser Institute. Born in Newfoundland in 1945, he received his B.A. (*summa*) at St. Francis Xavier University in 1966 and his Ph.D. in Economics at the University of Western Ontario in 1969. From 1969 to 1973, he worked in various research capacities at the Bank of Canada, Ottawa, and when he left in 1973 was Research Officer in charge of the Special Studies and Monetary Policy Group in the Department of Banking. Immediately prior to joining The Fraser Institute, Dr. Walker was Econometric Model Consultant to the Federal Department of Finance, Ottawa. Dr. Walker has also taught Monetary Economics and Statistics at the University of Western Ontario and Carleton University.

Dr. Walker was editor of, and a contributor to, thirteen of The Fraser Institute's previous books. In most recent years these have included: *Canadian Confederation at the Crossroads: The Search for a Federal-Provincial Balance* (1979); *Tax Facts* (1979, with Sally C. Pipes); *Unions and the Public Interest* (1980); *Rent Control: Myths & Realities* (1981); *Reaction: The National Energy Program* (1981, with G. Campbell Watkins), and *Discrimination, Affirmative Action, and Equal Opportunity* (1981, with Walter Block).

Dr. Walker is a regular economic commentator on national television and radio, and, in addition, addresses university students and a larger number of service and professional organizations on Canadian public policy issues.

SALLY C. PIPES

Sally C. Pipes is Assistant Director of the Vancouver-based Fraser Institute. Born in Vancouver, she graduated with a Bachelor of Arts in Economics from the University of British Columbia in 1967. Prior to joining The Fraser Institute in 1974, Mrs. Pipes held a variety of research positions in both the private and public sectors, including the Policy and Planning Branch, federal Department of Energy, Mines and Resources, and the Bureau of Economics of the provincial Ministry of Economic Development. In 1969, she joined the Employers' Council of British Columbia as a Research Economist and in 1973 became a member of the economics department of the Council of Forest Industries of British Columbia.

A Past President of the Association of Professional Economists of British Columbia she is currently President of the Canadian Association for Business Economics, a federation of six participating economics associations from Montreal to Vancouver.

She co-authored with Spencer Star *Income and Taxation in Canada, 1961-1975* and co-authored with Michael Walker *How Much Tax Do You Really Pay?* (1976) and *Tax Facts* (1979).

DAVID S. GILL

David Gill was born in 1953 in New Westminster, British Columbia. In 1976 he received his B.A. (Economics) from Simon Fraser University and in 1978 his M.A. (Economics) from the University of California at Los Angeles. With the exception of his dissertation, he has completed work towards his Ph.D in Economics at U.C.L.A. Mr. Gill is presently attending Law School at the University of British Columbia and following graduation in May 1982, will begin a nine-month appointment as a law clerk in the B.C. Supreme Court. "More on Unexpected Inflation and Unemployment," an article written by Mr. Gill and Geoffrey Newman was published in the *Atlantic Economic Journal* in the Fall of 1976.

Chapter 1
The Canadian Tax System

THE MANY FACES OF THE TAX COLLECTOR

Under the Canadian constitution the federal government and the provincial governments are essentially given unlimited powers of taxation. In the words of the British North America Act, the provinces are limited to the collection of taxes which are paid directly by the person being taxed—so-called *direct taxes*. But because of the broad judicial interpretation given to the meaning of "direct," the provinces have been able to levy all sorts of taxes except import duties and taxes on sales which cross provincial borders. Given this unlimited scope for taxation and the 100 years of ingenuity that have elapsed, it is not surprising that Canada now has a very complicated tax system.[1]

Some understanding of this complexity can be obtained simply by noting the twenty-one categories of tax set out in Table 1. This number has grown over the past few years as new taxes like the oil export charge and the airport tax have been implemented.

Income taxes predominate

It is evident from Table 1 and Figure 1 that personal income taxes are the largest single source of government revenue. During 1978 some 24.6 billion dollars were extracted by federal and provincial income tax—a sum which represented 32.2 per cent of the total taxes that Canadians pay.

TABLE 1
The Different Taxes Paid by Canadians and the Proportion that they Represent of the Total

Category of tax	1978 $ millions	1978 % of total taxes	1961 $ millions	1961 % of total taxes
Personal income tax	24,625.2	32.2	2,099.0	22.7
Sales tax	9,274.7	12.1	1,350.7	14.6
Profits tax	8,589.2	11.2	1,198.7	13.0
Property tax	7,578.1	9.9	1,285.2	13.9
Resources tax	5,562.9	7.3	265.7	2.9
Federal social security tax	2,006.0	2.6	388.0	4.2
Canada Pension Plan (inc. QPP)	2,721.0	3.6	0.0	0.0
Import duties	2,638.5	3.5	437.9	4.8
Auto, fuel, and gas tax	2,272.7	3.0	525.2	5.7
Provincial social security tax	2,148.6	2.8	155.0	1.7
Liquor tax	1,725.5	2.3	449.6	4.9
Hospital and medical premiums	1,648.5	2.2	120.4	1.3
Tobacco tax	1,323.9	1.7	387.0	4.2
Motor vehicle registrations	995.0	1.3	179.4	1.9
Other provincial fees, licence fees	870.2	1.1	10.8	.1
Municipal other business taxes	769.2	1.0	45.5	.5
Municipal other taxes and levies	533.1	.7	104.0	1.1
Provincial insurance premiums	210.5	.3	30.5	.3
Amusement and admission tax	97.1	.1	24.1	.3
Other federal excise taxes	829.0	1.1	28.0	.3
Succession and estate taxes	0.0	0.0	145.0	1.6

Source: Statistics Canada, Federal Government Finance, Provincial Government Finance, Local Government Finance, Catalogue Nos. 68-211, 68-207, 68-203, 1961 and 1962; 1978 and 1979. Revenue Canada, Statistical Services Division.

Figure 1 — Where Governments obtained their Revenue in 1961 and 1978

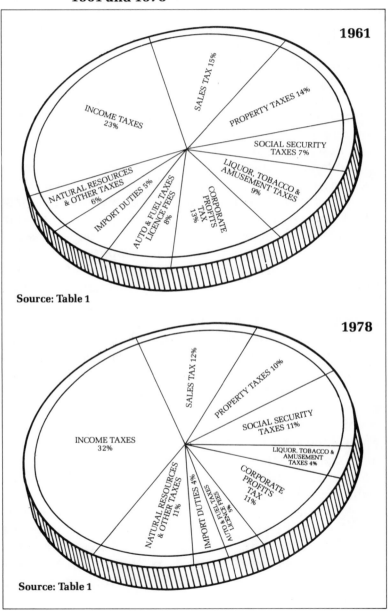

1961

SALES TAX 15%

INCOME TAXES 23%

PROPERTY TAXES 14%

SOCIAL SECURITY TAXES 7%

LIQUOR, TOBACCO & AMUSEMENT TAXES 9%

NATURAL RESOURCES & OTHER TAXES 6%

IMPORT DUTIES 5%

AUTO & FUEL TAXES LICENCE FEES 8%

CORPORATE PROFITS TAX 13%

Source: Table 1

1978

SALES TAX 12%

PROPERTY TAXES 10%

SOCIAL SECURITY TAXES 11%

INCOME TAXES 32%

LIQUOR, TOBACCO & AMUSEMENT TAXES 4%

CORPORATE PROFITS TAX 11%

NATURAL RESOURCES & OTHER TAXES 11%

IMPORT DUTIES 4%

AUTO & FUEL TAXES LICENCE FEES 5%

Source: Table 1

Second in line as a source of federal and provincial revenues was the sales tax—representing 12.1 per cent of tax
revenue and 9.3 billion tax dollars. Corporate profits taxes,
at 11.2 per cent of total taxes, accounted for a further 8.6
billion dollars, while property and natural resource taxes
accounted for 13.1 billion dollars and 17.2 per cent respectively. Together these five kinds of tax accounted for nearly
75 per cent of total government revenue during 1978. It is
interesting to note that both the corporate profits tax and
the income tax were implemented in 1916 and 1917 as
"temporary" measures to finance World War I.

Table 1 also illustrates how the Canadian tax structure
has evolved over the seventeen years since 1961. The most
obvious change has been the evolution of the personal
income tax. While always a prominent feature of the tax
system, the reader will note that the income tax has, in
recent years, become increasingly important. In 1961
income taxes represented only 22.7 cents out of every tax
dollar Canadians paid, but by 1978 income taxes
accounted for 32.2 cents—more than twice the revenue
generated by the second-running sales tax.

This radical increase came about largely through pas-
sive interaction between the progressive income tax system and money incomes swollen by inflation.[2] Until the
income tax was indexed to the inflation rate in 1974, all
income increases were taxed at progressively higher rates
in spite of the fact that much of the increased income
represented illusory inflation-based gains. This "income
tax bonanza" did not occur because of any legislated
changes in tax rates or through any specific action of the
Parliament of Canada.

As a consequence of this bonanza, government was
able to rely less on other forms of taxation and to allow the
burden of some of these taxes to fall. However, in some
important cases—notably sales tax and resource taxes—
the rate of tax was increased despite rapidly growing
revenues from personal income tax. (Table 2 presents the

TABLE 2

Total Taxes as a Percentage of Total Canadian Income

Category of tax	1978 %	1961 %
Personal income tax	13.8	6.4
Sales tax	5.2	4.1
Profits tax	4.8	3.7
Property tax	4.3	3.9
Resources tax	3.1	1.0
Federal Social Security Tax	1.2	1.2
Canada Pension Plan (inc. QPP)	1.5	0.0
Import duties	1.5	1.6
Auto, fuel and gas tax	1.3	1.4
Liquor tax	1.0	1.3
Other taxes	5.3	3.7
TOTAL	43.0	28.3

Source: See Table 1 and Statistics Canada, System of National Income and Expenditure Accounts, Catalogue No. 13-001, 1980 and 1961.

burden of the top ten taxes contributing to government revenue in 1978. The figures in the table are the effective rates of taxation relative to total Canadian income.)

Unlike income taxes, sales taxes are levied principally by the provincial governments—though the federal government has gradually increased its participation in this revenue source through such taxes as the federal manufacturers' sales tax. As a consequence, while revenue from the income tax explosion poured into the *federal* government's coffers, the *provinces* were led by their perceived need for tax revenue to gradually boost their sales tax rates (except for the province of Alberta which has no sales tax and in British Columbia where the sales tax has been adjusted up and down. It was reduced from 7 per cent to 5 per cent on April 11, 1978, on April 1, 1979 a further reduction to 4 per cent was made, but on March 10, 1981 it was increased to 6 per cent).

Increased resource taxation has resulted primarily from rises in the price of oil and gas, triggered by the oil embargo and subsequent cartelization of oil pricing by the

OPEC countries in 1973.[3] In the normal course of events these price rises in Canada would automatically have meant a sharp rise in the return to Canadian producers. But the reaction of provincial governments was to absorb much of this "windfall," or "rent," as it has been called, in the form of higher taxes or royalties. The federal government, for its part, imposed a further tax on producers who were exporting oil. (This tax, the oil export charge, amounted to the difference between the controlled Canadian price per barrel and the world price.) Proceeds from the federal tax were then used to subsidize imports of foreign oil into the eastern Canadian provinces. Federal oil tax collections from this source will fall steadily in the future because as existing oil export permits expire it is unlikely that they will be renewed.

In the period since 1974 both the provincial and federal governments have escalated their tax grab—but especially the federal government. The National Energy Program and the new Energy Agreement will allow the federal government to earn about 7 billion dollars from petroleum during 1982. Estimates suggest that this makes the federal government the most significant beneficiary of petroleum taxation.[4]

DIVIDING THE SPOILS

Another interesting feature of the present Canadian tax system is the extent of participation by the various levels of government, federal, provincial, and municipal. Table 3 provides a breakdown of major taxes by these different levels of government. It is clear from this table that provincial governments are rapidly becoming the dominant tax collectors. In 1961 provincial governments collected 32 per cent of total taxes in Canada, while federal and municipal governments collected 68 per cent. By 1978, however, provincial governments were collecting 42 per cent and the other levels only 58 per cent.

TABLE 3

Taxes Collected by Federal, Provincial, and Municipal Governments

(billions of dollars)

Category of tax	Federal 1978	Federal 1961	Provincial 1978	Provincial 1961	Municipal 1978	Municipal 1961
Personal income tax	14.0	2.0	10.6	.1	—	—
Sales tax	4.7	.3	4.6	1.0	—	—
Property tax	—	—	.1	.0	7.5	1.3
Profits tax	6.2	1.0	2.4	.2	—	—
Resources tax	.4	.0	5.2	.3	—	—
Social security tax	2.7	.4	1.4	.2	—	—
Canada and Quebec Pension Plans	2.0	—	.7	—	—	—
Import duties	2.6	.5	—	—	—	—
Liquor taxes	.6	.2	1.1	.2	—	—
Auto, fuel and gas taxes	.6	—	1.7	.4	—	—
Other taxes	1.5	.4	4.4	.5	1.3	.1
TOTAL	35.3	4.8	32.2	2.9	8.8	1.4

(per cent)

Category of tax	Federal 1978	Federal 1961	Provincial 1978	Provincial 1961	Municipal 1978	Municipal 1961
Personal income tax	57	95	43	5	—	—
Sales tax	51	23	49	77	—	—
Property tax	—	—	1	1	99	99
Profits tax	72	83	28	17	—	—
Resources tax	7	1	93	99	—	—
Social security tax	66	67	34	33	—	—
Canada and Quebec Pension Plans	74	—	26	—	—	—
Import duties	100	100	—	—	—	—
Liquor taxes	35	50	65	50	—	—
Auto, fuel and gas taxes	26	—	74	—	—	—
Other taxes	21	40	61	50	18	10
TOTAL	46	53	42	32	12	15

Source: See Table 1.

It must be acknowledged that the impression given by these figures is distorted somewhat by the fact that some of the revenue of municipal and provincial governments comes from other levels of government. For example, in 1961 fully 30 per cent of provincial and municipal revenues were derived from other levels of government. (Provinces received transfers from the federal government, while municipalities received transfers from both levels.)

In the case of provincial revenues, the figures for 1961 reflect the tax agreement that was in effect between the federal and provincial governments. Under the agreement the federal government "rented" the provinces' rights to tax personal incomes. In effect, the provinces relinquished their right to tax personal incomes in return for cash payments from the federal government which collected all the taxes.[5] Accordingly, the tax-collection statistics for 1961 do not reflect the *division* of the revenues produced but only which level of government actually *collected* them.

In 1978, the collection figures more closely matched the revenue divided between federal and provincial governments due to the fact that revenue-sharing agreements have been gradually modified to eliminate tax rental arrangements and shared-cost programs. In the years following 1978, the provinces have had, increasingly, to raise their own revenue. As a consequence, tax receipts by different levels of government will more closely reflect the actual sharing of tax revenues. To a considerable degree this evolution reflects the changing attitudes of the partners in Canadian confederation, and the changing tax arrangements are the harbinger of a more decentralized federation. (In the case of Quebec, separate tax collection facilities have been in existence for some time.)

The relationship between provincial and municipal government revenues reflects a different process. Municipalities now collect much less of their total revenue in the form of taxes than they did in 1961. And, in fact, fully 47 per cent of municipal revenue is now accounted for by transfers from federal and provincial governments — mainly the latter. In part, the emerging role of municipalities as dependencies of the provincial government is a result of decreasing reliance on property taxation as a form of finance (see Table 1). Property taxes accounted for only 9.9 per cent of total taxes (of all kinds) in 1978 as opposed to 13.9 per cent in 1961. Over the same period, property taxes shrank from 14 per cent of the total tax burden in 1961 to only 10 per cent in 1978 (see Figure 1).

This trend toward less reliance on property taxation contrasts sharply with the situation in the United States and in California, in particular, where the sudden increase in property taxation touched off what has been called the "Proposition 13" movement. The failure of similar initiatives in Canada may be directly attributable to the different strategy of local government finance pursued in this country. Moreover, there has recently been a move in at least one Canadian province (British Columbia) to place a ceiling on municipal spending — a manoeuvre aimed directly at the tax appetite of local governments.

THE FIFTH COLUMN

Hidden taxation

Most people are aware of the fact that they pay income tax, sales tax and property tax, the so-called direct taxes. Many others, appropriately, regard the various social security levies like unemployment insurance contributions and Canada and Quebec Pension Plan payments, as taxes. Similarly, many families know how much of these taxes they pay, either in terms of the rate (in the case of provincial sales taxes) or the total amount (in the case of property and income taxes). There are, however, many taxes of which Canadians, by and large, are unaware. These taxes are built into the price of goods and services but are not identified to the final consumer as a tax cost. For want of a better name, we call these *implicit* or *hidden taxes*.

Figure 2—Government Take from a Litre of Gasoline

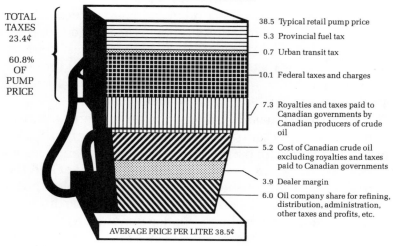

VANCOUVER
PUMP PRICE
REGULAR GASOLINE

TOTAL
TAXES
23.4¢

60.8%
OF
PUMP
PRICE

38.5 Typical retail pump price

5.3 Provincial fuel tax

0.7 Urban transit tax

10.1 Federal taxes and charges

7.3 Royalties and taxes paid to Canadian governments by Canadian producers of crude oil

5.2 Cost of Canadian crude oil excluding royalties and taxes paid to Canadian governments

3.9 Dealer margin

6.0 Oil company share for refining, distribution, administration, other taxes and profits, etc.

AVERAGE PRICE PER LITRE 38.5¢

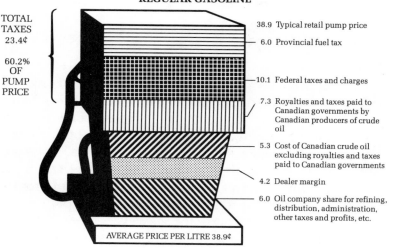

TORONTO
PUMP PRICE
REGULAR GASOLINE

TOTAL
TAXES
23.4¢

60.2%
OF
PUMP
PRICE

38.9 Typical retail pump price

6.0 Provincial fuel tax

10.1 Federal taxes and charges

7.3 Royalties and taxes paid to Canadian governments by Canadian producers of crude oil

5.3 Cost of Canadian crude oil excluding royalties and taxes paid to Canadian governments

4.2 Dealer margin

6.0 Oil company share for refining, distribution, administration, other taxes and profits, etc.

AVERAGE PRICE PER LITRE 38.9¢

Source: The High Cost of Our Cheap Oil, The Canadian Manufacturers' Association

Figure 2—Government Take from a Litre of Gasoline

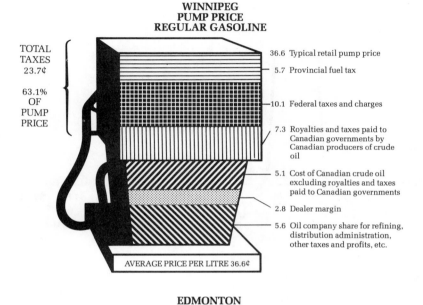

**WINNIPEG
PUMP PRICE
REGULAR GASOLINE**

TOTAL
TAXES
23.7¢

63.1%
OF
PUMP
PRICE

36.6 Typical retail pump price

5.7 Provincial fuel tax

10.1 Federal taxes and charges

7.3 Royalties and taxes paid to
Canadian governments by
Canadian producers of crude
oil

5.1 Cost of Canadian crude oil
excluding royalties and taxes
paid to Canadian governments

2.8 Dealer margin

5.6 Oil company share for refining,
distribution administration,
other taxes and profits, etc.

AVERAGE PRICE PER LITRE 36.6¢

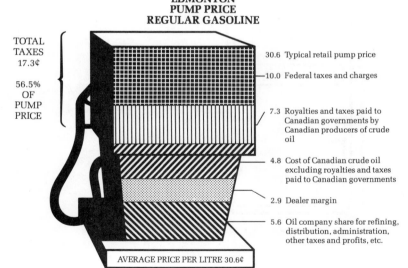

**EDMONTON
PUMP PRICE
REGULAR GASOLINE**

TOTAL
TAXES
17.3¢

56.5%
OF
PUMP
PRICE

30.6 Typical retail pump price

10.0 Federal taxes and charges

7.3 Royalties and taxes paid to
Canadian governments by
Canadian producers of crude
oil

4.8 Cost of Canadian crude oil
excluding royalties and taxes
paid to Canadian governments

2.9 Dealer margin

5.6 Oil company share for refining,
distribution, administration,
other taxes and profits, etc.

AVERAGE PRICE PER LITRE 30.6¢

**Source: The High Cost of Our Cheap Oil, The Canadian Manufacturers'
Association**

Figure 3—Government Take from a Bottle of Liquor

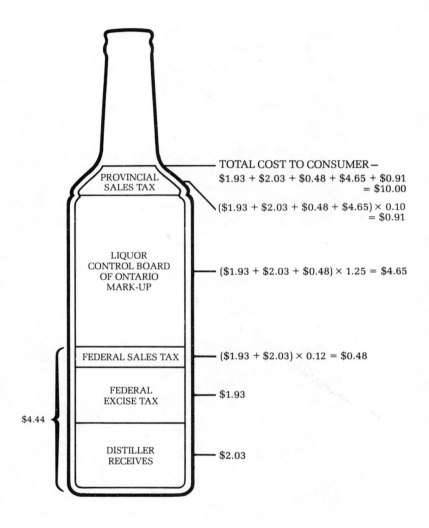

TOTAL COST TO CONSUMER—
$1.93 + $2.03 + $0.48 + $4.65 + $0.91
= $10.00

PROVINCIAL SALES TAX
($1.93 + $2.03 + $0.48 + $4.65) × 0.10
= $0.91

LIQUOR CONTROL BOARD OF ONTARIO MARK-UP
($1.93 + $2.03 + $0.48) × 1.25 = $4.65

FEDERAL SALES TAX
($1.93 + $2.03) × 0.12 = $0.48

FEDERAL EXCISE TAX
$1.93

$4.44

DISTILLER RECEIVES
$2.03

Source: Association of Canadian Distillers

Indirect taxes

There are several different kinds of hidden tax. Most well-known of these are the so-called *indirect taxes* — principally excise taxes on such items as tobacco and alcohol, manufacturers' sales taxes, and import duties. These taxes are paid by some intermediary in the production process and become incorporated in the final price of the product. The most notorious examples are tobacco, liquor and gasoline taxes. (See Figures 2 and 3 for a breakdown of taxes paid on a gallon of gasoline and a bottle of liquor.) In the case of liquor, the actual indirect rate of tax is about 99.73 per cent; in the case of cigarettes, it is 136.96 per cent.[6] The final consumer of both of these products pays the taxes without them having been identified as such. Of course, most people are aware that alcohol and tobacco are highly taxed, even if they do not know the actual rate of tax.

During 1978, total indirect taxes of all kinds amounted to 29.3 billion dollars in Canada. This was 15 per cent of total Canadian income and accounted for 33 per cent of total government revenue. In other words, quite apart from the tax they pay when they *receive* their incomes, Canadians pay, on average, a further 15 per cent in indirect taxes when they *spend* their income. Furthermore, about one-third of all government revenue is collected in this indirect — hidden — form.

The hot potatoes — passing tax forward

Needless to say, from the point of view of the individual, any tax that can be avoided is money in his or her pocket. As a result people throughout the economy are constantly attempting to avoid situations in which they will have to pay taxes, and seeking to pay as little tax as possible, whatever their situation. The moonlighting tradesman who engages in "cash only" transactions; the mechanic who fixes his neighbour's truck in return for free cartage; the dentists who fix fellow dentists' families' teeth on a reciprocal basis; the tycoon whose business is "incorpo-

---

Figure 4 — Take-Home Pay versus Gross Pay

In 1980 an employee in Ontario with $14,520 in taxable income had to get an increase of 13.0 per cent, or $2,414 in gross pay, to realize a 9 per cent increase in after-tax pay. Tax rates vary by province and comparable figures for the other provinces are presented in the table below.

Per cent wage increase required

(Take-home pay at $14,520)

Nfld.	P.E.I.	N.S.	N.B.	Que.
13.8%	13.4%	13.4%	13.4%	15.3%

Ont.	Man.	Sask.	Alta.	B.C.
13.0%	13.5%	13.5%	12.8%	13.0%

Source: Canadian Tax Foundation, *The National Finances*, 1980-81 Table 4-9, p. 69.

---

rated" in the Grand Cayman Islands: all have in common their desire to avoid "giving the government a piece of the action."

By the same token, the average Canadian employee measures his welfare in terms of after-tax dollars, and in each new wage bargain aims to get an increase in take-home pay. The fact that an increase in gross terms will imply a smaller increase in after-tax dollars motivates the employee or his union representative to demand a larger gross increase. By doing so, the employee is attempting to get the employer to bear the burden of the additional tax. For an example of this process see the box insert — Figure 4.

Expressed slightly differently, the employee who bargains in this manner is attempting to "pass the tax forward." His behaviour is not unique but, on the contrary, is a general characteristic of all employees of the Canadian economy. Corporations, for example, attempt to pass their higher profits and payroll taxes forward to the consumer in the form of higher prices (as well as backward on employees in the form of lower wages). Of course, all of these attempts may or may not be successful in any single instance, and they will be accomplished to varying degrees through time.

Who pays the indirect taxes?

In order to calculate the actual tax bill paid by a family, it is necessary to determine how much indirect tax it pays. But since those from whom the tax is *collected* attempt to pass the tax along to others, it is difficult to know where the burden of these taxes ultimately lies. For example, a general sales tax is collected by and remitted to government by retailers. It is clear, however, that in most cases the retailers do not actually bear the tax — they are merely the agents for collecting it. The actual effect of the tax is to increase the price of all goods and services affected by the tax and to cause a corresponding reduction in the purchasing power of family incomes. Accordingly, to the extent that a general sales tax causes an increase in the general level of prices, the tax is borne not by the collectors but by income earners in the economy whose incomes now buy less.

Payroll taxes such as unemployment insurance premiums and Canada and Quebec Pension Plan contributions are collected in part from the employer and in part from the employee. And, while no one would dispute the fact that the employee pays the employee portion, in most cases it is true that the employee will also pay the so-called employer's portion. This is so because the payroll tax paid by the employer reduces the total amount of money the employer has available to pay labour-related costs. In other words, payroll taxes reduce potential wage and salary payments below what they otherwise would have been. Since no corresponding reduction can be expected in the price of the products that the employee will want to purchase, the payroll tax in effect burdens the employee.

While both of these arguments have been framed in terms of employees and their wages and salaries, it is clear that taxes burden capital income as well. For example, a general sales tax reduces the purchasing power of all income, not just wage and salary income. As a result, it is appropriate to view the general sales tax burden as falling on all forms of income, including interest income and dividends. All of the tax burden estimates constructed in this study therefore allocate the burden of general sales taxes in proportion to all income received by a family. In practical terms, this means that if general sales taxes amount to 6 per cent of total Canadian income in a particular year, we would add 6 per cent of a family's total income to the family's tax bill when we calculate how much tax the family pays.

In computing this tax burden, income that a family receives from government is explicitly ignored. The reason for this is that the payments received from government, such as the Old Age Pension, have historically been and are currently either directly or indirectly indexed to the general level of prices (that is, increased to offset the effects of inflation). As the general price level rises, in step with the sales tax, the purchasing power of such transfers from government as Family Allowance and Old Age Security payments is not permitted to fall. As a consequence, the general sales tax does not have the effect of burdening income received from government (transfers), and it would be inappropriate to allocate any part of the burden of general sales taxes to this sort of income.[7]

While the burden of a general sales tax and payroll taxes is relatively straightforward to assign, the assignment of particular excise taxes is a little more elusive. Whereas a general sales tax increases all prices and hence reduces the purchasing power of all incomes, particular taxes on commodities usually affect only the price of that commodity. For example, excise taxes imposed on liquor, motor vehicles, and fuels affect only the prices of those products, in the first instance at least. (Ultimately, of course, they may affect a whole range of prices — fuel taxes affect the price of transportation, as do motor vehicle taxes. These taxes may therefore have an overall effect although levied only on a particular product.)

In the light of these considerations, it has been the usual practice when calculating tax burdens to allocate the burden of particular excise taxes according to the consumption of those items. The 1976 tax burden studies published by the Fraser Institute employed this methodology.[8] However, following this methodology gives rise to a variety of problems. First of all, only the first round effects of the excise tax are incorporated and, hence, the actual distribution of the tax burden may differ substantially from the estimate. Secondly, this method may not even provide good estimates of the first round effects of the tax. This is so because the relative burden of a particular tax borne by a family is determined not by the family's consumption of the taxed item but by the fraction of the family's income spent on the item relative to the national average.[9]

In view of these problems with the traditional approach, and given that the *proportions* of income spent on different items by various income groups do not vary widely from the average, we decided for the purposes of this study to distribute excise taxes in the same way as general sales taxes. That is to say, it is assumed that excise taxes burden total incomes — excluding government transfers to persons.

So, the answer to the question, Who pays the indirect taxes? is a straightforward one. Although indirect taxes appear in a variety of forms, they ultimately burden the income that the family earns.

OTHER TAXES BY OTHER NAMES

In addition to "formal" taxes levied by government, there are a variety of other government actions which, while having the same effect as taxes, are not normally identified as such. These activities are becoming an increasingly important feature of the Canadian economic landscape and must receive special mention.

Clothing and textile taxes

In November 1976, the federal government imposed a quota on imported clothing and textiles. Its purpose was to limit the importation of inexpensive clothing and textiles and so protect Canadian markets for Canadian clothing and textile manufacturers. The associated decline in competition for the Canadian consumer's clothing expenditure dollar will undoubtedly have produced a higher price for clothing than would otherwise have existed (particularly since world-wide clothing and textile markets are in a depressed state owing to expanded output from Far Eastern producers).

The difference between the price for clothing that would have prevailed in the absence of the quota and the price that actually prevails is a tax on the consumer. Proceeds from this tax go directly to producers and are, in effect, a producer subsidy. There is no difference in principle between this sort of tax and the other hidden taxes that we have been discussing. Of course, these "clothing taxes" do not show up in government revenue figures, and precise estimates of their size are difficult to make, but we cannot ignore their existence. R.J. and P. Wonnacott in their book *Free Trade Between the United States and Canada* have estimated that the total amount of tax levied in the form of tariff protection or other barriers to international competition may be as high as 10.5 per cent of

Canada's Gross National Product.[10] Currently, this amounts to a tax of some 27.3 billion dollars.

Marketing board taxes

At present, there are some 177 farm products' cartels in Canada. These cartels or marketing boards generally have the effect of suppressing competition in the production of the cartelized product, and they consequently cause the price of the product to be higher than it otherwise would have been. As in the case of clothing and textiles, the amount by which the marketing board price exceeds the price that would prevail in its absence—that is, in the market—is a tax on the consumer. Accordingly, marketing boards ought to be viewed as a device for transferring money from consumers to producers. And this transfer is equivalent to a tax on consumers, the proceeds of which are given to producers.

The increasing power of marketing boards, and the seeming reluctance of government to restrain their growth (the federal Minister of Agriculture actually fosters their growth), suggests that these marketing board taxes will become increasingly important in Canada. Moreover, as restraint in government taxation and spending becomes a reality, it will become increasingly expedient for government to rely on hidden "regulatory" taxation of this sort.

Regulatory taxation

In general, a government can achieve a given objective either by taxation and subsidization or by regulation— rather than imposing import quotas, the federal government could have assisted Canadian clothing manufacturers by giving them a direct subsidy financed from general tax revenue. That the government chooses to use regulation to convey a subsidy in this fashion should not distract attention from the fact that a subsidy has been provided, and that it is the Canadian consumer who pays for it.

Deferred taxation

During his budget statement in November 1978, Mr. Chrétien, former federal Minister of Finance, made much of the fact that because the personal income tax structure had been indexed to inflation, there had, in effect, been a reduction in personal income taxation compared to what would have prevailed in the absence of indexing. That is to say, exemptions had been increased by the rate of inflation and tax brackets had been shifted to ensure that incomes swollen by inflation would not be taxed more heavily on that account alone. While this change in the tax structure, first introduced in 1974, was indeed a welcome one, it would be naive to uncritically accept the move as a permanent reduction in the government's propensity to tax.

In fact, the "reduction" in personal income tax revenues was accompanied — starting in 1975 — by deficits and shortfalls in the federal government's cash position which were unprecedented in peacetime.

Although this situation is not entirely attributable to the decline in personal income tax revenues, it is clearly the case that continued growth in income taxation would have meant a slightly smaller deficit and a reduction in net cash requirements to be financed by issuing debt. Accordingly, in assessing Canada's current level of taxation, it is appropriate to take into account the extent to which tax collections are merely *deferred* by current tax "reductions."

In other words, when calculating the total tax burden of all government operations in a given year, it is appropriate to include not only current taxes levied but also future taxes which must be levied to discharge debts acquired by the government in the current year. To the extent that government finances its operations by deficit financing or issuing bonds — deferred taxation — there is a hidden tax burden implicit in its operations. In Chapter 4 we have calculated estimates of the total tax burden which include all of these deferred taxes.

How Much Tax Should Canadians Pay?

In 1917 when he first introduced the Personal Income Tax, the Finance Minister of the day, Sir Thomas White, was of the opinion that no Canadians should pay tax on income less than $2,000 if they were single and had no dependents. Married taxpayers, he said, should pay tax on income in excess of $3,000. The tax structure that ultimately evolved provided that single Canadians pay income tax on income in excess of $1,500, while married Canadians were exempted from the tax until their incomes exceeded $3,000. However, in the very next year, this was reduced to $2,000 for a married taxpayer and $1,000 for single Canadians.†

While the tax structure has gone through many changes in the intervening years, it is interesting to ask how Canadians would be treated for tax purposes in 1980-81 if this initial view of "ability to pay" had kept pace with developments in people's incomes. To answer this question we have adjusted the original exemption levels by the increase in average wages over the period since 1917. This adjustment yields an exemption level for 1980 of $5,764 for single taxpayers and $11,529 for married taxpayers. But actual personal exemptions for single and married taxpayers amounted to $2,890 and $6,500 in 1980 — in each case just over half the level that would have been allowed if the 1917 standard had continued in force.

The reason for the disparity is that over the years from 1917 to 1974 exemption levels were not indexed to the cost of living or the increase in family incomes — in fact, in a few years during the depression, exemption levels were actually *reduced*. Since 1974, exemption levels have been indexed to the rate of inflation.

†House of Commons Debates, July 25, 1917, p. 3765.

Chapter 2
Personal Income Taxation in Canada

We alluded to the fact in Chapter 1 that income taxes are the largest single source of government revenue. It therefore follows that the largest single tax paid by the average Canadian family is the income tax. As we also noted in Chapter 1, this tax came into existence in 1917 as a "temporary" emergency measure to help finance the increasing debt associated with World War I. "Nothing," it is said, "endures like the temporary."

THE 1981 INCOME TAX STRUCTURE

Table 4 presents the actual rates of income tax (both federal and provincial) encountered by the average single individual at various taxable income levels. As the figures show, the minimum rate of tax is 2.64 per cent payable on taxable income of $1.00. The maximum rate is payable at income levels of $118,981 or higher and amounts to 61.92 per cent of every dollar earned beyond that income level. These rates are the marginal rates of tax that a person encounters as he or she moves from one level of taxable income to the next. An equally interesting series of calculations relates to the amount of tax an individual theoretically pays on a given amount of total income (not taxable income), taking into account the standard deductions to which he or she is entitled. (Taxable income equals total income minus total deductions.) These rates are shown in Table 5.

TABLE 4

1980 and 1981 Combined Federal and Provincial
Personal Income Tax—Marginal Rates*

Taxable Income	1980	Taxable Income	1981
$ 1	2.64	$ 1	2.64
904	7.04	993	7.04
1,807	7.48	1,984	7.48
3,613	25.92	3,967	25.92
5,419	27.36	5,950	27.36
7,223	27.36	7,934	27.36
9,031	30.24	9,916	30.24
10,833	30.24	11,900	30.24
12,643	31.05	13,882	31.05
14,446	31.05	15,866	31.05
16,255	33.75	17,848	33.75
18,057	33.75	19,832	33.75
19,867	37.80	21,814	37.80
21,668	37.80	23,798	37.80
25,285	43.20	27,763	46.08
27,086	46.08	29,747	46.08
43,345	51.84	47,593	51.84
45,139	51.84	49,577	51.84
70,435	56.16	77,338	56.16
72,224	56.16	79,322	56.16
108,361	61.92	118,981	61.92
162,497	61.92	178,472	61.92
225,690	61.92	247,877	61.92
406,236	61.92	446,177	61.92
722,192	61.92	793,202	61.92

Source: Canadian Tax Foundation, *The National Finances, 1980-81*, Chapter 4, Table 4-4, p. 59.

*Tax rate which comes into effect with each additional amount of income.

In the case of a family, the situation can be slightly different because of deductions permitted for the dependent spouse. Support of children also eases somewhat the tax burden on the taxpayer. In perusing tax rates for the average family of four presented in Table 6, the reader should bear in mind the fact that this schedule of rates is not directly applicable for many families. In many cases

TABLE 5

Personal Income Tax Paid (Single Taxpayer—No Dependents) at Selected Levels of Income, 1980

Total Income Assessed	Total Tax Payable (Federal plus Provincial)	Tax Rate (average)
$ 7,500	$ 648	8.6%
10,000	1,270	12.7
12,500	1,912	15.3
15,000	2,624	17.5
17,500	3,368	19.2
20,000	4,144	20.7
25,000	5,876	23.5
30,000	7,831	26.1
50,000	17,206	34.4
100,000	44,234	44.2
200,000	105,448	52.7

Source: Canadian Tax Foundation, *The National Finances, 1980-81*, Chapter 4, Table 4-11, p. 71.

TABLE 6

Personal Income Tax Paid (Married Taxpayer—Two Dependent Children under Sixteen Years of Age) at Selected Levels of Income, 1980

Total Income Assessed	Total Tax Payable (Federal plus Provincial)	Tax Rate (average)
$ 7,500	—	—
10,000	$ 460	4.6%
12,500	1,067	8.5
15,000	1,719	11.5
17,500	2,431	13.9
20,000	3,186	15.9
25,000	4,785	19.1
30,000	6,600	22.0
50,000	15,624	31.2
100,000	42,501	42.5
200,000	103,536	51.8

Source: Canadian Tax Foundation, *The National Finances, 1980-81*, Chapter 4, Table 4-12, p. 72.

TABLE 7

Tax Rates and Number of Earners, 1980

Total Family Income	One Income Earner		Two Equal Income Earners	
	Total Income Tax Paid	Tax Rate on Total Income	Total Income Tax Paid	Tax Rate on Total Income
$ 15,000	$1,815	12.8%	$ 1,296	8.6%
20,000	3,342	16.7	2,540	12.7
25,000	4,981	19.9	3,824	15.3
30,000	6,855	22.9	5,248	17.5
50,000	16,018	32.0	11,752	23.5
100,000	42,977	43.0	34,412	34.4
200,000	107,515	53.8	88,468	44.2

Source: Canadian Tax Foundation, *The National Finances 1980-81*, Chapter 4, Table 4-11, 4-4, and calculations by the authors.

both adult members of the family declare taxable income. In this case they each file a separate return, and tax rates for individuals apply. Of course, this is to the advantage of the taxpayers. If, for example, a childless couple who are both working have the same income — say $15,000 per year — they pay total tax of about $5,248 when they file as individuals. If their total income of $30,000 were earned by only one of them, their total tax payable would be about $6,855 — a difference of $1,607.

In other words, if their income is earned by one family member, the family pays a gross tax rate of 22.9 per cent, but if their income is composed of two salaries the tax rate is only 17.5 per cent. The difference between the two tax rates rises as the family income increases until very high income levels are reached (see Table 7). This difference between the single and double income-earner family will continue to haunt the calculations in the remainder of this book. In particular, income tax payments shown in the various composite tax tables in Chapter 3 reflect the fact that, on average, tax payments are made by a mixture of single and double taxpayer families.

WHO PAYS THE INCOME TAX BILL?

While it is possible to calculate tax rates and amounts of tax payable on an "up-to-date" basis, analysis of the income tax system as a whole has to be based on two-year-old statistics. This arises because Revenue Canada processes its data with a one-year lag. Accordingly, our analysis of who pays the income tax — and of other related questions — must be based on the 1978 data. For the most part, however, we can rest assured that the relative magnitudes involved will be stable over time and, hence, that conclusions reached are reliable for 1982.

In 1978, a total of 24.1 billion dollars was paid by individuals in income taxes and, as Table 8 shows, nearly half of it was paid by individuals with incomes below $20,000. Individuals with incomes below $30,000 paid fully 71 per cent of the total income tax bill. In fact, 50 per cent of all income taxes were paid by individuals with incomes in the relatively narrow range, $12,000 to $25,000.

As column 4 of Table 8 shows, over half of all taxable returns were filed by individuals with incomes less than $10,000. This proportion reflects the large number of part-time workers, students employed during the summer, and other intermittent workers earning modest incomes. These taxpayers generated only 5 per cent of total tax revenue, while the top 15 per cent of taxpayers — those declaring income of $20,000 or more — contributed 58 per cent of the total income tax bill.

An interesting aspect of the information in Table 8 is the relationship between taxes paid and income declared. For example, as noted above, 42 per cent of the total income tax bill was paid by individuals with incomes below $20,000. From column 6 we discover that this group of indivuals earned 62 per cent of all the income declared. So, income earners below $20,000 paid a smaller proportion of the total tax bill than their share of total earned income might suggest. On the other hand, the top 15 per

TABLE 8

An Analysis of Income, Taxes, and Tax Returns by Income Class, 1978

Total Income Assessed	Col 1. Percentage of Total Tax Paid by Income Class	Col. 2 Percentage of Total Tax Paid by All Classes at or below this Class Level	Col. 3 Percentage of Total Returns Filed by this Income Class	Col. 4 Percentage of Total Returns Filed by All Classes at or below this Class Level	Col. 5 Percentage of Total Income Declared by this Income Class	Col. 6 Percentage of Total Income Declared by All Classes at or below this Class Level
Less than $4,000	.00	.00	27.27	27.27	3.72	3.72
4,000-4,999	.00	.00	5.05	32.32	2.07	5.79
5,000-5,999	.10	.10	4.80	37.12	2.40	8.19
6,000-7,999	1.30	1.40	9.08	46.20	5.79	13.98
8,000-9,999	3.46	4.86	8.94	55.14	7.32	21.30
10,000-11,999	5.31	10.17	7.94	63.08	7.95	29.25
12,000-14,999	10.46	20.63	10.03	73.11	12.27	41.52
15,000-19,999	21.76	42.39	12.86	85.97	20.27	61.79
20,000-24,999	17.77	60.16	6.93	92.90	14.03	75.82
25,000-29,999	11.18	71.34	3.22	96.12	7.97	83.79
30,000-39,999	11.07	82.41	2.32	98.44	7.17	90.96
40,000-49,999	4.86	87.27	.73	99.17	2.94	93.90
50,000-99,999	8.07	95.34	.70	99.87	4.17	98.07
100,000-199,999	2.88	98.22	.11	99.98	1.24	99.31
200,000 and over	1.78	100.00	.02	100.00	.69	100.00

Source: Taxation Statistics, Revenue Canada Taxation, Ottawa, 1980.

cent of taxpayers, who had incomes in excess of $20,000, paid about 58 per cent of the total tax bill while receiving only 38 per cent of total income earned.

The reason for this, of course, is the fact that the income tax structure is "progressive." That is, it takes a larger fraction from high incomes than it does from low incomes, as is clear from the tax rates presented in Table 7.

GET IT FROM THE RICH

It is often said, and more often believed, that the key to "social welfare" or "social justice" is the redistribution of income. That is, take income from those who have much and give it to those who have little. The extreme form of this prescription is the formula "from each according to his ability [to pay?] and to each according to his need" — the rule advanced in the *Communist Manifesto*.[1]

Our analysis in the preceding section of who pays the income tax reveals that Canada as a country already engages in significant taxation of those who are relatively well-off. However, a recent publication has suggested that Canada has *not* been successful in redistributing income from the rich to the poor — that ours is not a "Robin Hood" society.[2] It therefore remains interesting to ask whether or not we could achieve a more equal distribution of the benefits of the Canadian good-life by taxing more of the income of the richest Canadians.

How rich is rich?

The question that immediately arises is "How rich is rich?" At what level of income should the government tax away *all* increases in the interest of "equitable" income distribution? In view of the fact that Members of Parliament earn in excess of $30,000 per year, it is unlikely that "Canadians" would find it equitable to confiscate earnings less than that level. Let us, then, for the sake of illustration, select $30,000 as the maximum income that Canadians should be allowed to earn. Under this rule, all incomes above that level would be subject to a 100 per cent rate of income tax, and the proceeds would be distributed to all income earners with incomes less than $30,000.

Counting the rich

In 1978, 556,325 persons filed tax returns reporting income of $30,000 or more. Total income reported by these people was 19.6 billion dollars. If the government had really taxed away all income beyond $29,999, total tax revenue in 1978 would have been 5.6 billion dollars higher than it actually was. Redistribution of this increased tax revenue to those (13.7 million people) with incomes less than $30,000 would yield an average annual payment of $408.75 for each person submitting a tax return.

Taxing the "rich" not the source of wealth

This calculation is an important one because it reveals the practical impossibility of "getting it from the rich and redistributing it to the poor." Those who are impatient with the speed at which the economic process improves the condition of the poorest members of society ought to reflect on the fact that the same total increase in the incomes of those earning less than $30,000 would be achieved by about 5.1 per cent growth in total incomes *even if it were distributed in exactly the same way as it is currently.*

Chapter 3
How Much Tax
Do You Really Pay?

The issues discussed in Chapter 2 focus on the income tax bill that Canadians pay. But income tax represents less than half of the total taxes paid by the average Canadian family. The purpose of this chapter is to expand the analysis of taxation to include all taxes that Canadians pay. Tables 13 and 14 at the end of the chapter enable the reader to calculate his or her own total income and total tax bill for 1980. (Complete income and tax tables for each of the provinces are included as an appendix.)

HOW MUCH INCOME DO YOU REALLY EARN?

Cash income

In order to properly calculate how much tax a person (or a group) pays, it is necessary first to determine their income. While this process may seem simple, what a person's income *seems* to be is very different from what it *actually* is. This section of the chapter, therefore, explains the method for deriving the income figures used in subsequent sections.

The ultimate goal of income calculations is to determine the total income a Canadian citizen would have if there were no taxes of any sort and other factors remained unchanged. To arrive at such a figure it is necessary to discover all the income sources a person might have, to determine the taxes that might have been paid on this income *before* the person received it, and finally to add up all of the income taxes.

The first layer of income items is easily discovered: wages, salaries, interest from savings bonds, rent from the in-law suite in the basement, or even rent on "the back forty." These sorts of items comprise what in this study is called *cash income*.

Full cash income and underreporting

In its regular surveys of household income, Statistics Canada finds that people typically omit some income items when they estimate their cash income — that is they under-report their income. The particular items omitted vary from family to family, but, on average, families tend to underestimate their total income by from 4 to 12 per cent. Items that might be omitted include miscellaneous interest income, income from "moonlighting," and so on. Fortunately, Statistics Canada does have a comprehensive measure of income in the National Accounts framework, and it is therefore possible not only to *know* that the survey information is incorrect but also to adjust that information to make it more accurate.[1] Accordingly, the *full cash income* estimates used in this study have been adjusted to make them consistent with the comprehensive income figures contained in the National Accounts. In interpreting the results, in light of his or her own circumstances, the reader should use the *cash income* figure as the key income figure. The *full cash income* corresponding to it has been calculated and is displayed in all of the relevant tables.

It may be useful at this stage to provide an example based on a fictitious individual. In order to make the example as comprehensive as possible, it is assumed that the individual involved in the example has income from all of the sources identified in the study — an unlikely circumstance for any real individual. The example is presented in Table 9.

Total income

In addition to cash income most families also have various

TABLE 9

Full Cash Income, 1980

Category	$
Wages and salaries	19,165
Income from farm operations	462
Unincorporated non-farm income	936
Interest	1,121
Dividends	130
Private Pension payments	534
Family Allowance*	406
Old Age pension	325
Government pension payments*	119
Other transfers from government*	1,468
Equals	
Full cash income	24,666

*Income from government is commonly referred to as a "negative tax" or a "transfer payment."

forms of non-cash income that must be included in a comprehensive income figure. For example, most wage and salary earners receive fringe benefits as a condition of their employment. Also part of an employee's income is the investment accumulated by his or her pension plan and the interest accumulated — though not paid — on his or her insurance policy.

At a higher level of subtlety, a comprehensive income total should also include a number of other income sources. For example, a homeowner is, in effect, his or her own landlord. Therefore, the homeowner receives rental income. Because this implicit income is not paid in cash, its existence must be "imputed" or assigned to the home-owner.

The reason for including such income in a comprehensive income measure is that the homeowner could actually earn that income by renting the premises to somebody else. On the same basis income is imputed for the rental of farm properties. Income is also imputed on

TABLE 10

Total Income, 1980

Category	$
Full cash income	24,666
Plus	
Fringe benefits from employment	1,559
Investment income of insurance companies	209
Investment income of trusteed pension plans	185
Imputed interest	200
Value of food from farms	14
Corporate retained earnings	453
Bad debts	23
Equals	
Total income	27,309

account of interest-free loans that people make. The interest foregone is in fact implicit income in the form of a gift.

Profits not paid out as dividends by corporations but held in the form of retained earnings are in fact income of the shareholders of the corporation, even though they do not receive it in the year in which it is reported. Also, bad debts which are written off by corporations are in fact a source of net income to the debtor and are treated as such. Finally, food consumed by farm operators is evaluated at market price and attributed to farm operators as income.

Again to make the calculation clear, the total income figure is accumulated in Table 10 for a fictitious individual who is assumed to have income from all sources.

Total income before tax

Some of the income earned by Canadians is taxed before they receive it. For example, shareholders receive dividends on corporate profits after corporate profit taxes have been paid. In the absence of taxes, the dividends (or retained earnings) of the shareholder would have been higher. Therefore, in order to arrive at a *total income before tax,* it is necessary to add back the corporate profits collected from corporations. Similarly, if there were no property taxes, net after-tax rental income would be higher than it actually is. Therefore, before-tax income must be augmented by the amount of property taxes paid.

In the discussion of indirect and hidden taxes in Chapter 1, it was noted that these taxes reduce the effective income available to Canadians because they increase the price of items that people buy with their incomes. In effect, income after tax is less, in terms of the things it will buy, than it was before tax. In order to arrive at an estimate of before-tax income it is necessary, therefore, to add back to incomes the reduction brought about by indirect taxes.

Finally, payroll taxes levied on firms are, as noted earlier, effectively paid by employees, because the taxes reduce the amount of money available to pay wages and salaries. Accordingly, it is necessary to add back the amount of payroll taxes to employees' incomes to arrive at a before-tax total income estimate.

Table 11 presents an example of a complete income calculation for a fictitious individual who is assumed to have income from all of the income sources identified in the study and to have paid all of the identified taxes.

CALCULATING THE TOTAL TAX BILL

Basically, the tax calculation for the average Canadian family consists of adding up the various taxes that the family pays. Hidden taxes such as taxes on tobacco and alcohol are allocated according to the method indicated in Chapter 1. To preserve consistency, the family used, by way of example, in the tax calculation in Table 12 is the same family used in the income calculation. Readers who have an interest in their own income and tax situation (or that of their neighbour) for 1980 can refer to Tables 13 and 14. An appendix at the end of the book contains income and tax tables for each of the provinces.

TABLE 11

Total Income Before Tax, 1980

Category	$
Wages and salaries	19,165
Income from farm operations	462
Unincorporated non-farm income	936
Interest	1,121
Dividends	130
Private pension payments	534
Family Allowance	406
Old Age Pension	325
Government pension payments	119
Other transfers from government	1,468
Equals	
Full cash income	24,666
Plus	
Fringe benefits from employment	1,559
Investment income of insurance companies	209
Investment income of trusteed pension plans	185
Imputed interest	200
Value of food from farms	14
Corporate retained earnings	453
Bad debts	23
Equals	
Total income	27,309
Plus	
Payroll taxes	1,430
Property taxes	749
Profit taxes	886
Indirect taxes	3,311
Equals	
Total income before tax	33,685

Source: Tables 9-11, Fraser Institute Canadian Tax Simulator (CANTASIM).

Table 12

Tax Bill of the Average Canadian Family, 1980

Category	$
Family cash income	22,500
Full cash income	24,666
Total income	27,309
Total income before tax	33,685
Taxes	
Income taxes	3,345
Profit taxes	886
Sales taxes	1,432
Liquor, tobacco, amusement, and other excise taxes	469
Auto, fuel, and motor vehicle license taxes	399
Social security, medical, and hospital taxes	1,485
Property tax	749
Natural resources taxes	647
Import duties	403
Other taxes	491
Total taxes	10,306
Taxes as a percentage of: Family cash income	45.8%
Total income before tax	30.6%

Source: Fraser Institute Canadian Tax Simulator (CANTASIM).

TABLE 13

1980 Income Table for Canada

Your Cash Income	Your Full Cash Income	Income from Government	Hidden Income	Hidden Purchasing Power Loss	Total Income Before Tax
		(Dollars per family)			
5000	6744	4308	654	1531	8930
5500	7515	4606	773	1756	10044
6000	8131	4712	951	1991	11073
6500	8747	4819	1129	2226	12102
7000	9327	4926	1138	2491	12956
7500	9898	5034	1105	2764	13767
8000	10469	5141	1072	3037	14578
8500	11035	5185	1072	3294	15401
9000	11580	5004	1191	3496	16267
9500	12125	4824	1310	3698	17133
10000	12670	4643	1429	3900	17999
10500	13215	4462	1548	4101	18865
11000	13719	4268	1682	4272	19673
11500	14168	4056	1836	4401	20404
12000	14616	3844	1990	4529	21136
12500	15065	3632	2144	4658	21867
13000	15514	3420	2298	4787	22599
13500	15995	3336	2329	4894	23219
14000	16497	3331	2283	4988	23769
14500	16999	3327	2237	5082	24318
15000	17501	3322	2191	5176	24868
15500	18003	3317	2145	5271	25418
16000	18505	3313	2099	5365	25968
16500	18981	3247	2105	5443	26529
17000	19443	3145	2141	5511	27096
17500	19905	3043	2178	5580	27663
18000	20367	2942	2214	5648	28230
18500	20830	2840	2250	5717	28797
19000	21292	2739	2287	5786	29364
19500	21754	2637	2323	5854	29931
20000	22216	2535	2360	5923	30498
20500	22678	2434	2396	5991	31065
21000	23140	2332	2433	6060	31633
21500	23646	2323	2501	6164	32311
22000	24156	2320	2572	6270	32998
22500	24666	2318	2643	6376	33685
23000	25176	2315	2714	6482	34372
23500	25686	2313	2785	6588	35059
24000	26195	2310	2856	6694	35746
24500	26705	2308	2927	6800	36433

TABLE 13 continued

Your Cash Income	Your Full Cash Income	Income from Government	Hidden Income	Hidden Purchasing Power Loss	Total Income Before Tax
		(Dollars per family)			
25000	27215	2305	2998	6906	37120
25500	27725	2302	3070	7012	37807
26000	28235	2300	3141	7119	38494
26500	28744	2297	3212	7225	39181
27000	29254	2295	3283	7331	39868
27500	29753	2281	3392	7492	40637
28000	30250	2266	3506	7659	41414
28500	30747	2251	3619	7825	42192
29000	31245	2236	3732	7992	42969
29500	31742	2220	3846	8158	43746
30000	32240	2205	3959	8325	44523
30500	32737	2190	4072	8491	45300
31000	33234	2175	4185	8658	46078
31500	33732	2160	4299	8824	46855
32000	34229	2145	4412	8991	47632
32500	34727	2130	4525	9158	48409
33000	35224	2115	4638	9324	49186
33500	35776	2115	4760	9477	50012
34000	36334	2116	4882	9628	50843
34500	36892	2118	5004	9778	51675
35000	37451	2119	5126	9929	52506
35500	38009	2121	5248	10080	53338
36000	38567	2123	5371	10231	54169
36500	39126	2124	5493	10382	55000
37000	39684	2126	5615	10533	55832
37500	40242	2127	5737	10684	56663
38000	40801	2129	5859	10835	57495
38500	41359	2131	5981	10986	58326
39000	41917	2132	6104	11136	59158
39500	42517	2136	6348	11368	60233
40000	43123	2141	6607	11610	61339
40500	43728	2145	6867	11851	62445
41000	44333	2149	7126	12093	63552
41500	44938	2154	7385	12335	64658
42000	45543	2158	7645	12576	65765
42500	46149	2162	7904	12818	66871
43000	46754	2167	8164	13060	67977
43500	47359	2171	8423	13301	69084
44000	47964	2176	8683	13543	70190
44500	48570	2180	8942	13785	71296
45000	49175	2184	9202	14026	72403

Source: Statistics Canada on Income.

TABLE 14

1980 Tax Table for Canada

Your Cash Income	Profits Tax	Income Tax	Sales Tax	Liquor, Tobacco, Amusement and Other Excise Taxes	Auto, Fuel & Motor Vehicle Licence Taxes	Social Security, Pension, Medical & Hospital Taxes	Property Tax	Natural Resources Taxes	Import Duties	Other Taxes	Total Taxes
						(Dollars per family)					
5000	439	37	138	47	39	399	386	293	40	96	1915
5500	497	53	163	55	46	475	437	333	47	113	2218
6000	546	108	194	66	55	548	474	385	57	130	2562
6500	596	162	226	77	64	621	511	438	66	146	2906
7000	669	192	253	86	72	602	568	497	74	157	3170
7500	748	217	280	95	80	560	630	558	82	169	3415
8000	826	241	306	105	87	519	691	618	90	176	3660
8500	895	286	335	115	96	498	748	666	99	188	3927
9000	929	403	376	131	108	552	786	666	112	207	4271
9500	963	519	416	147	121	606	824	667	126	227	4615
10000	997	636	456	163	133	659	862	667	139	246	4959
10500	1031	753	497	178	145	713	900	667	152	266	5304
11000	1053	870	540	193	158	760	926	663	165	282	5610
11500	1058	985	586	208	171	799	934	651	177	295	5864
12000	1063	1101	633	222	184	838	942	639	189	308	6118
12500	1067	1216	679	236	196	876	950	627	202	321	6372
13000	1072	1332	726	250	209	915	958	616	214	334	6626
13500	1070	1440	765	263	221	945	955	617	224	345	6845
14000	1062	1543	801	275	231	968	945	627	234	355	7041
14500	1055	1646	836	286	241	992	935	637	244	364	7238
15000	1047	1749	872	298	251	1016	925	648	254	374	7434

TABLE 14 continued

(Dollars per family)

Your Cash Income	Profits Tax	Income Tax	Sales Tax	Liquor, Tobacco, Amusement and Other Excise Taxes	Auto, Fuel & Motor Vehicle Licence Taxes	Social Security, Pension, Medical & Hospital Taxes	Property Tax	Natural Resources Taxes	Import Duties	Other Taxes	Total Taxes
15500	1040	1852	907	310	261	1039	915	658	264	384	7631
16000	1033	1955	943	322	271	1063	905	668	274	393	7827
16500	1019	2059	980	333	281	1092	890	670	284	401	8011
17000	1003	2164	1019	345	291	1124	873	668	294	408	8188
17500	986	2268	1057	356	301	1156	855	666	304	414	8365
18000	970	2372	1096	368	311	1188	838	664	315	421	8542
18500	953	2477	1135	380	321	1220	820	662	325	427	8719
19000	936	2581	1173	391	331	1252	802	660	335	434	8896
19500	920	2685	1212	403	341	1284	785	658	345	440	9073
20000	903	2790	1251	414	351	1316	767	656	355	447	9250
20500	887	2894	1289	426	361	1348	750	653	365	454	9427
21000	870	2998	1328	438	371	1380	732	651	375	460	9604
21500	874	3113	1363	448	381	1415	737	650	384	470	9835
22000	880	3229	1397	459	390	1450	743	648	393	481	10071
22500	886	3345	1432	469	399	1485	749	647	403	491	10306
23000	892	3460	1467	480	408	1520	756	645	412	502	10541
23500	898	3576	1501	490	418	1555	762	644	421	512	10776
24000	903	3692	1536	501	427	1590	768	642	430	523	11012
24500	909	3807	1571	511	436	1625	775	641	439	533	11247
25000	915	3923	1606	522	445	1660	781	639	448	544	11482
25500	921	4039	1640	532	455	1695	788	638	457	554	11718
26000	927	4154	1675	543	464	1730	794	636	466	564	11953
26500	933	4270	1710	553	473	1765	800	635	475	575	12188
27000	939	4386	1744	564	482	1800	807	633	484	585	12423
27500	960	4511	1777	575	491	1837	819	664	494	598	12726
28000	983	4636	1810	586	500	1875	832	698	503	610	13035

28500	1005	4762	1843	597	509	1914	845	732	513	623	13343
29000	1028	4888	1875	609	518	1952	858	766	522	636	13652
29500	1051	5014	1908	620	526	1990	871	800	532	648	13961
30000	1074	5139	1941	631	535	2028	885	834	541	661	14269
30500	1096	5265	1973	642	544	2066	898	868	551	674	14578
31000	1119	5391	2006	654	553	2104	911	902	560	686	14887
31500	1142	5517	2039	665	562	2142	924	936	570	699	15196
32000	1165	5642	2071	676	571	2180	937	970	580	712	15504
32500	1188	5768	2104	687	580	2219	950	1004	589	724	15813
33000	1210	5894	2137	698	588	2257	963	1038	599	737	16122
33500	1235	6029	2171	709	598	2297	984	1048	608	753	16431
34000	1259	6164	2205	719	607	2338	1006	1055	617	769	16740
34500	1283	6300	2239	730	616	2378	1028	1061	626	786	17049
35000	1308	6436	2273	740	625	2419	1050	1068	635	803	17358
35500	1332	6572	2308	751	634	2460	1073	1075	644	819	17667
36000	1357	6708	2342	761	644	2500	1095	1082	653	836	17976
36500	1381	6844	2376	772	653	2541	1117	1088	662	852	18285
37000	1405	6980	2410	782	662	2581	1139	1095	671	869	18594
37500	1430	7116	2444	793	671	2622	1161	1102	680	885	18903
38000	1454	7252	2478	803	680	2663	1183	1108	689	902	19212
38500	1479	7387	2513	813	690	2703	1205	1115	698	918	19521
39000	1503	7523	2547	824	699	2744	1227	1122	707	935	19830
39500	1559	7641	2582	834	707	2771	1278	1151	716	954	20194
40000	1620	7757	2618	844	716	2796	1332	1182	725	973	20565
40500	1681	7873	2654	854	725	2821	1387	1214	734	993	20935
41000	1741	7988	2689	865	733	2846	1441	1246	743	1013	21306
41500	1802	8104	2725	875	742	2871	1496	1278	752	1032	21677
42000	1862	8220	2761	885	750	2897	1550	1309	761	1052	22047
42500	1923	8336	2797	895	759	2922	1604	1341	770	1072	22418
43000	1983	8451	2832	905	767	2947	1659	1373	779	1091	22789
43500	2044	8567	2868	915	776	2972	1713	1405	788	1111	23159
44000	2104	8683	2904	926	785	2997	1768	1436	797	1130	23530
44500	2165	8799	2939	936	793	3022	1822	1468	806	1150	23901
45000	2226	8914	2975	946	802	3048	1876	1500	815	1170	24271

Source: Statistics Canada Data on Taxes.

Chapter 4
The Canadian
Consumer Tax Index

As noted in preceding chapters, Canada's system of taxation is enormously complex. This complexity makes it extremely difficult to describe the tax system in a simple way — difficult to provide a few concise numbers or words to characterize it at a given point in time. Any discussion of the tax system — even a simplified one — is likely to be complicated because the system has so many different aspects. As we showed in Chapter 1, even counting the number of taxes is a difficult business. Also complicated is the pattern of tax rates — who pays what — and, of course, the changes in these factors over a period of time. In fact, this book attempts to provide a simplified description of how the tax system is evolving — and, natural pride of authorship notwithstanding, this is not a simple book.

Why construct a Consumer Tax Index?

For individual taxpayers, the most interesting variable for Canadians is how much tax they actually have to pay. In 1976, when we wrote the Fraser Institute's first tax study, *How Much Tax Do You Really Pay?*, we devised an index which we called the *Consumer Tax Index*. Its purpose was to provide a summary-at-a-glance indicator of what has been happening to the tax bill faced by the average Canadian family over the years since 1961.

    Some readers of that book found the tax index too simple — it failed to take into account how the tax money was spent by governments and, therefore, showed only one side of the ledger.[1] On the other hand, the index in that first study and in our second, *Tax Facts*, was widely used by financial and consumer affairs columnists across the country to describe how the Canadian tax system had evolved. Moreover, it has been in continuous use ever since its release and has been described as the most up-to-date measure of the extent of Canadian taxation. It was particularly widely cited during the summer of 1978 in the wake of the California tax revolt — the so-called "Proposition 13" movement.

While it is easy to acknowledge that any single measure of something as complex as the Canadian tax system is bound to be incomplete, it is our view that the Canadian Consumer Tax Index is a useful and important indicator of a very important economic burden. Moreover, it remains the only widely available measurement of its kind. In this spirit we shall continue to calculate and publish the Consumer Tax Index and other associated statistics, in our ongoing assessment of the Canadian tax system.

What is the Canadian Consumer Tax Index?

The Consumer Tax Index is an index of the total dollar tax bill paid by the average Canadian family. It is constructed by calculating the tax bill of an average Canadian family for each of the years included in the index. The index below therefore shows the tax bill for a family with an income of $5,000 in 1961, for a family with an income of $8,000 in 1969, and so on. Now, while *each* of these families was average, in an income sense, in each year selected, it is not necessarily the same family. The objective is not to trace the tax experience of a particular family but rather to plot the experience of a family which was average in each year.

The index thus answers the question "How has the tax burden of the average family changed since 1961, bearing in mind the fact that the average family has changed in that

TABLE 15

Taxes Paid by the Average Canadian Family, 1961-1980

Year	Your Cash Income $	Full Cash Income $	Total Income before Tax $	Taxes Paid $	Increase in Taxes Paid over Base Year %
1961	5,000	5,643	7,582	1,675	—
1969	8,000	8,448	11,323	3,117	86.1
1972	10,000	10,690	14,154	4,203	150.9
1974	12,500	13,353	17,976	5,429	224.1
1976	16,500	17,607	21,872	5,979	257.0
1978	18,500	20,298	27,627	8,343	398.1
1980*	22,500	24,666	33,685	10,306	515.3

Source: Data for the years 1961-1978 were calculated from the Fraser Institute tax tables.

*Estimates for 1980 are based on separate estimates of the 1980 income, tax, and family distributions.

period?" To be clear about some of the questions the index will not answer, we can note that the average family in 1980 was headed by a younger person, was more likely to own a car, less likely to own a house, and had fewer members than the average family in 1961. Most important, the family's earned income more than tripled over the period.

The basis of the tax index is the total tax calculation presented in Table 15. Income and tax calculations were made for a selection of years beginning in 1961 and culminating in 1980. (As information becomes available in the future, we shall publish the index to include later years. We hope to be able to provide the reader with the Consumer Tax Index every two years.) The tax bill of the average family yielded by this process was then converted to index form. The results are reported in Table 16 and Figure 5. They show that the tax bill of the average Canadian family has increased by 515 per cent over the period since 1961, and that the index had a value of 615 in 1980.

At least part of that increase reflects the effects of inflation. In order to eliminate the effects of the declining

TABLE 16

The Canadian Consumer Tax Index
1961=100

Year	Index*
1961	100.0
1969	186.1
1972	250.9
1974	324.1
1976	357.0
1978	498.1
1980	615.3

Source: Table 15.

*The Index is constructed from the "Taxes Paid" column in Table 15. To calculate the Index, the taxes in each year are divided by the figure in the base year, in this case 1961, and then multiplied by 100.

TABLE 17

The Consumer Tax Index Based on 1971 Dollars of
Purchasing Power

Year	Real Value of Taxes Paid	Per cent Increase in Taxes Paid over Base Year
1961	$2,233.3	—
1969	3,312.4	48.3
1972	4,010.5	79.6
1974	4,343.2	94.5
1976	4,015.4	79.8
1978	4,762.0	113.2
1980	4,893.6	119.1

Source: See Table 15 and Statistics Canada, The Consumer Price Index, Catalogue No. 62-001, Table 2.

value of the dollar, we have also calculated the tax index in real dollars—that is, dollars of 1971 purchasing power. While this adjustment has the effect of reducing the steepness of the index's path over time, the real-dollar tax index, nevertheless, increased by 119 per cent over the period (see Table 17).

Figure 5 — The Canadian Consumer Tax Index
1961-1980

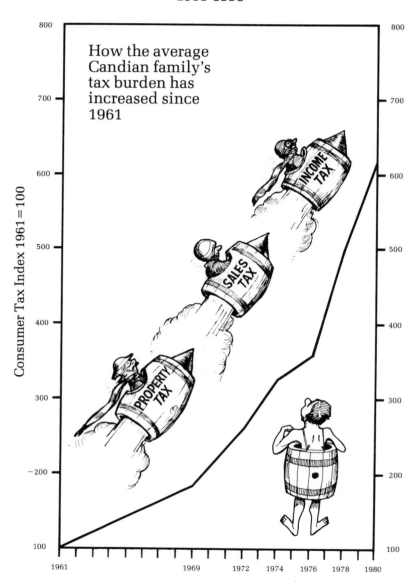

How the average Candian family's tax burden has increased since 1961

Consumer Tax Index 1961 = 100

Source: Table 16

TABLE 18

The Consumer Tax Index Versus
the Balanced Budget Tax Index

Year	Consumer Tax Index	Balanced Budget Tax Index
1961	100.0	100.0
1969	186.1	204.3
1972	250.9	281.1
1974	324.1	368.5
1976	357.0	398.4
1978	498.1	581.9
1980	615.3	719.0

Source: Table 19.

What the Consumer Tax Index shows

The dramatic increase in the Canadian tax index over the period 1961-1980 was produced by the interaction of a number of factors. First, there was a dramatic increase in incomes over the period, and even with no change in tax rates the family's tax bill would have increased substantially. In the absence of a change in the tax rate, growth in family income alone would have produced an increase in the tax bill from $1,675 in 1961 to $7,537 in 1980. The second contributing factor was a 38 per cent increase in the tax rate faced by the average family.

In recent years, commencing in 1975, the rate of increase in the tax bill has slowed appreciably, reflecting a decline in the overall rate of taxation and an increase in the extent to which all governments are resorting to issuing debt — that is, bonds — to finance their expenditures. This phenomenon shows up most clearly in a comparison of the Consumer Tax Index and the Fraser Institute's new *Balanced Budget Tax Index*. The latter includes the debt that is being acquired by the various levels of government on the grounds that, if the governments' budgets were in fact balanced and no debt were issued, the tax bill would have been higher by the amount of the debt issued. The debt

issued by such Crown Corporations as electric power
authorities is not included in this calculation since, in a
case of this kind, future electricity rates or other prices —
rather than tax rates — will reflect the cost of the debt.

This comparison of the two indices in Table 18 and
Figure 6 shows that if governments were to balance their
budgets the tax bill of the average family would be very
much higher than it actually is. To the extent that Canadians are made to feel better off by the apparent decline in tax
rates, ignoring the accumulating debt acquired by government, they are being subjected to a colossal fiscal illusion.

TAXES VERSUS THE NECESSITIES OF LIFE

While the Consumer Tax Index does show the way in
which the average family's tax bill has changed over the
past nineteen years, that information becomes even more
significant when it is compared to other family commit-
ments. Accordingly, in this section the tax bill is compared
with other major expenditures of the average Canadian
family — for food, shelter, and clothing.

Table 19 and Figure 7 compare the average dollar
amount of family cash income, total income before tax,
and total taxes paid with family expenditures on other
items such as food, shelter, and clothing. It is clear from
these figures not only that taxation has become the most
significant item that consumers face in their budgets but
also that it is growing more rapidly than any other single
item. This is made more evident in Table 20 and Figure 8,
which show the various items as indices based on 1961
values. While incomes rose during the period from 1961 to
1980 by 344.3 per cent, prices rose 181.0 per cent, food
expenditures rose 267.8 per cent, shelter by 333.9 per cent,
and clothing 297.2 per cent, the tax bill of the average
family grew by 515.3 per cent. The balanced budget tax
rate grew even more rapidly, rising by 619.0 per cent over
the same period.

Table 21 and Figure 9 present the same information
but expressed as percentages of total income before tax. In

Figure 6 — The Canadian Consumer Tax Index versus The Balanced Budget Tax Index 1961-1980

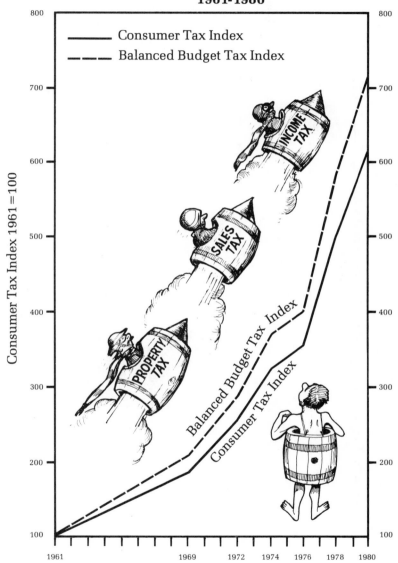

TABLE 19

Income, Taxes, and Selected Expenditures of the Average Canadian Family (dollars)

Year	Income		Taxes		Selected Expenditures†		
	Average cash income	Total income before tax	Average taxes paid	Average taxes paid (including deficits)	Average shelter expenditures	Average food expenditures	Average clothing expenditures
1961	5,000	7,582	1,675	1,675	977	1,259	435
1969	8,000	11,323	3,117	3,422	1,294	1,634	654
1972	10,000	14,154	4,203	4,708	1,778	1,791	739
1974	12,500	17,976	5,429	6,172	1,983	2,320	886
1976	16,500	21,872	5,979	6,673	2,709	2,838	1,119
1978	18,500	27,627	8,343	9,746	3,283	3,319	1,250
1980*	22,500	33,685	10,306	12,044	4,239	4,631	1,728

Source: Statistics Canada Urban Family Expenditure, 1978-1961, Catalogue Nos. 62-549, 62-547, 62-544, 62-541, 62-537, 62-535, 62-525, and 62-001 Prices and Price Indices.

†All selected expenditure items include indirect taxes.

*Estimates for 1980 are based on separate estimates of the 1980 income, tax, and family distributions.

Figure 7 — Taxes and Selected Expenditures of the Average Canadian Family, 1961-1980

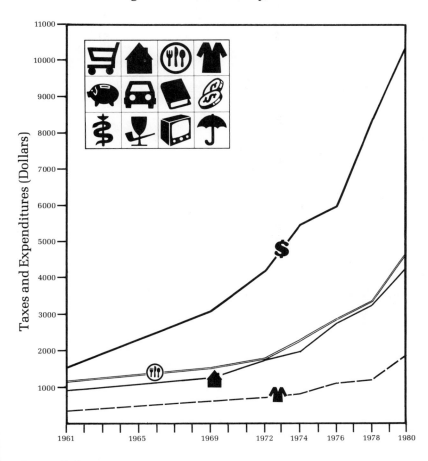

Source: Table 19

TABLE 20

Indices of Income, Taxes, and Selected Expenditures of the Average Canadian Family
1961 = 100

Year	Taxes		Income	Consumer Prices	Selected Expenditures†		
	Consumer tax index	Consumer tax index (including deficits)	Total income before tax index	Consumer price index	Average shelter expenditure index	Average food expenditure index	Average clothing expenditure index
1961	100.0	100.0	100.0	100.0	100.0	100.0	100.0
1969	186.1	204.3	149.3	125.5	132.4	129.8	150.3
1972	250.9	281.1	186.7	139.8	182.0	142.3	169.9
1974	324.1	368.5	237.1	166.8	203.0	184.3	203.7
1976	357.0	398.4	288.5	198.7	277.3	225.4	257.2
1978	498.1	581.9	364.4	233.7	336.0	263.6	287.4
1980*	615.3	719.0	444.3	281.0	433.9	367.8	397.2
Per cent Increase 1961-1980	515.3	619.0	344.3	181.0	333.9	267.8	297.2

Source: The figures in this table are converted to indices by dividing each series in Table 19 by its value in 1961 and then multiplying that figure by 100.

†All expenditure items include indirect taxes.

*Expenditure data for 1980 are trend estimates.

Figure 8 — How the Canadian Consumer Tax Index (CTI) has increased, relative to other Selected Indices, 1961-1980

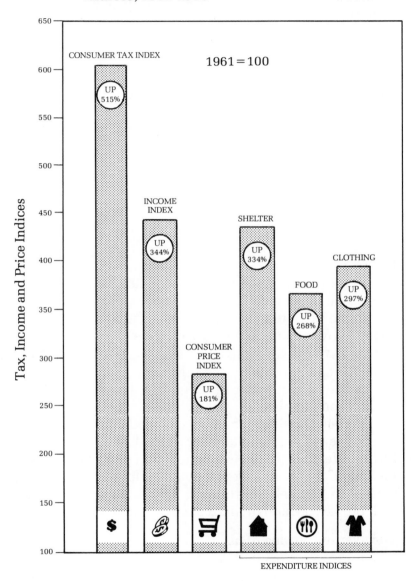

Source: Table 20

TABLE 21

Taxes and Selected Expenditures of the Average Canadian Family Expressed as a Percentage of Total Income Before Tax (per cent)

Year	Taxes	Selected Expenditures†		
		Shelter	Food	Clothing
1961	22.1	12.9	16.6	5.7
1969	27.5	11.4	14.4	5.8
1972	29.7	12.6	12.7	5.2
1974	30.2	11.0	12.9	4.9
1976	27.3	12.4	13.0	5.1
1978	30.2	11.9	12.0	4.5
1980*	30.6	12.6	13.7	5.1

Source: Table 19.

†All selected expenditure items include indirect taxes.

*Expenditure data for 1980 are trend estimates.

this form, the data reveal some interesting comparisons. For example:

• In 1961 the average family had to use 35.2 per cent of its income to provide itself with food, shelter, and clothing. In the same year, 22.1 per cent of the family's income went to government in the form of taxes.

• By 1974 the situation had been reversed, and 30.2 per cent of income went to satisfy the taxman, while only 29 per cent was required to provide the family with food, shelter, and clothing.

• In 1980 the situation again changed, and the average family spent a higher fraction of its income on the necessities of life than it did on taxes. However, as we have indicated above, this development is partly an illusion created by tax deferral through deficit financing by federal, provincial, and municipal governments.

The average burden of tax versus the average family's tax burden

This chapter has dealt exclusively with the tax position of the average family. To some extent the conclusions of such an analysis can be misleading, because of the exclusive

Figure 9 — Taxes and Selected Expenditures* of the Average Canadian Family Expressed as a Percentage of Total Income Before Tax

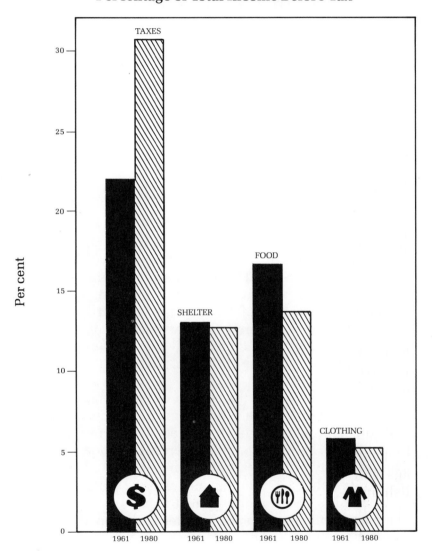

* All selected expenditure items include indirect taxes.

Source: Table 21

TABLE 22

Average Tax Rates for All Canadian Families Versus Tax Rates of the Average Canadian Family
(per cent)

Year	Average Canadian Family's Tax Rate		Average Tax Rate for All Canadian Families	
	Excluding debt	Including debt	Excluding debt	Including debt
1961	22.1	22.1	25.2	25.2
1969	27.5	30.2	31.1	34.3
1972	29.7	33.3	31.6	35.5
1974	30.2	34.3	33.3	37.8
1976	27.3	30.5	31.8	35.9
1978	30.2	35.3	31.0	35.0
1980	30.6	35.8	31.4	35.4

Source: Fraser Institute Canadian Tax Simulator (CANTASIM).

focus on the average family. In the next chapter this weakness is corrected by discussing the tax position of "unaverage" Canadians. Similarly, it is possible to mistake the average family's burden for another measure which is sometimes used, that of the average tax burden of all Canadian families. Before leaving discussion of the average family's tax burden, therefore, it is important to establish and understand the differences between these two measures.

In this chapter, the tax burden of the average family has been calculated by selecting an average-income family and calculating that family's theoretical tax burden from the tax tables. In this regard it is interesting to note that the average family in 1980 had an income of $22,500 and that the family paid $3,345 in income tax or 32 per cent of its total tax bill. The remaining $6,961 or 68 per cent was made up of other taxes such as sales and property taxes. Another way of calculating an average tax burden would be to add up all the taxes in the economy and simply divide that total tax figure by total incomes in the economy. This would produce an average tax rate for all Canadian families. Such a calculation is displayed in Table 22 along with the average family's tax rate. This table also shows what the tax rates would have been if the deficits incurred by governments were included.

It is quite clear from the table that the average family's tax rate is below that faced by all Canadians in the economy as a whole. Moreover, as the analysis in the next chapter shows, the tax rate faced by the average family is considerably lower than the tax rates faced by families whose incomes are above average. Similarly, much of the total tax bill is collected from families whose incomes are above the average. For example, in 1978, 56 per cent of the tax bill was collected from families with incomes above the income of the average family ($18,500).

It is this "progressivity" of the tax structure which produces the difference between the two average tax calculatons — the more progressive the tax system the greater the difference. This "progressivity" is the subject of discussion in the next chapter.

Chapter 5
The Relative Burden of Tax

In Chapter 4 we investigated the tax burden of the average Canadian family and how that burden has changed through time. While that view of the tax system has some inherent interest, it represents a very particular aspect of a much larger picture. The purpose of this chapter is to examine the larger picture — to examine all income groups and how their relative income and tax positions have changed over the time span between 1961 and 1978.

THE DISTRIBUTION OF INCOME

In order to analyze the relative income and tax positions of Canadians we have divided all Canadian families into ten groups or deciles. This was accomplished by arranging families according to total income before tax from lowest to highest and then selecting the first 10 per cent (lowest incomes), the second 10 per cent, and so on. The resulting grouping of families is presented in Table 23.

The table reveals that the relative shares of the different income groups have been remarkably constant over the period since 1961. In evaluating this result, the reader should bear in mind that the data have a variety of aspects that make them susceptible to misinterpretation. First of all, the data fail to make any allowance for the age of the individuals. This is an important fact, since age is a principal determinant of income. Young people first entering the labour market typically earn wages or salaries considera-

TABLE 23

Decile Distribution of Income
(per cent)

Year	Lower Income Groups			Middle Income Groups				Upper Income Groups		
	1st	2nd	3rd	4th	5th	6th	7th	8th	9th	10th
1961	2.6	2.6	5.6	7.0	8.1	9.1	11.3	11.5	14.9	27.2
1969	1.6	2.9	4.9	6.2	7.7	8.7	10.3	12.3	15.2	30.0
1972	1.0	3.3	4.7	6.2	7.5	8.9	10.4	12.7	15.8	29.4
1974	1.0	2.8	4.6	6.2	7.5	9.2	10.3	13.3	15.6	29.8
1976	1.2	3.0	4.6	5.9	7.1	8.9	9.8	13.2	16.5	29.8
1978	1.3	3.0	4.9	6.6	8.0	9.1	10.9	12.7	15.7	28.0

Source: Fraser Institute Canadian Tax Simulator (CANTASIM).

TABLE 24

Income in Age Group as a Percentage of Average for All Groups, Male Canadian, 1978

Age	Taxation Statistics Data	Statistics Canada Income Survey Data	Average Profile
under 25	.593	.612	.603
25-34	1.042	.973	1.008
35-44	1.293	1.207	1.250
45-54	1.289	1.270	1.280
55-64	1.108	1.060	1.084
65 & over	.627	.582	.605

Source: Statistics Canada Income Distribution by Size in Canada, 1978, Catalogue No. 13-207; Revenue Canada, Taxation Statistics, 1980 Edition, Analyzing Returns for the 1978 Taxation Year and Miscellaneous Statistics.

bly below the average and considerably below their own lifetime average. Similarly, elderly people who have passed the age of retirement are typically in a phase of their life when their incomes are considerably below their lifetime average and when they are spending the savings and pensions of their working lifetime.

For example, Table 24 displays the "life-cycle average expected wage" for a Canadian male in 1978. Two sources of data on the earnings profile are available—information from taxation statistics and Statistics Canada's income surveys. While the two sources yield different estimates, they both show the expected age-related movement in wages relative to the average.

Failure to account for the age of income earners can lead to a considerably distorted impression of how income distribution is changing—particularly if there are dramatic changes in the age structure of the population. And it must be noted that such dramatic changes have recently occurred in Canada's population.

In 1961, the first year covered by Table 23, fully 75 per cent of the workforce were in their prime earning years—between 25 and 64 years of age. By 1978, the number of

people in the workforce at that stage in their lives consti-
tuted only 62 per cent of the workforce. In other words, the
1961 distribution of income includes 25 per cent of the
population who had not yet attained or who had passed
their earnings peak. By contrast a full 38 per cent of those
included in the 1978 figures were at these stages in their
lives.

A second important warning for those who would
draw from these data conclusions about the "equity" of the
income distribution is that they ignore income-in-kind
that people receive from government. Housing, medical
care, education, and other services which are received as
direct benefits from government, rather than in the form of
cash payments, are not reflected in the income distribution table. And the public provision of these services
potentially represents one of the most significant redistri-
butive aspects of Canadian society.

For these reasons it would be inappropriate to infer
from the data in Table 23 that there had been no change in
the effective distribution of income since 1961. The data in
its present form is incapable of providing meaningful
answers to that question. What the data does provide is a
yardstick against which to measure the distribution of
taxes. It will allow us to infer whether, for example, groups
of people with modest incomes bear a disproportionate
share of the tax burden. It will also permit us to construct
tax rates for families, ranging from those with the lowest
incomes to those with the highest incomes. This will
provide an indication of the progressivity or regressivity
of the Canadian tax burden. In order to arrive at these
results it is necessary to combine income results with
those on tax distribution which are the subject of the next
section.

TAX DISTRIBUTION AND TAX RATES

Our measurements of the distribution of the tax burden
provide some interesting and, indeed, puzzling results for

TABLE 25

Decile Distribution of Taxes
(per cent)

Year	Lower Income Groups			Middle Income Groups				Upper Income Groups		
	1st	2nd	3rd	4th	5th	6th	7th	8th	9th	10th
1961	2.1	2.1	4.5	5.7	6.7	7.7	10.5	10.7	14.6	35.6
1969	1.1	2.0	4.0	5.3	6.9	7.7	9.4	11.8	15.0	36.9
1972	0.6	1.9	3.5	5.1	6.7	8.4	9.8	12.4	16.1	35.5
1974	0.6	1.8	3.7	5.1	6.7	8.4	9.6	13.0	15.9	35.5
1976	0.6	1.9	3.6	5.1	6.0	7.6	8.6	12.9	17.3	36.3
1978	0.7	2.2	4.2	6.2	7.7	8.8	10.8	13.0	16.6	30.0

Source: Fraser Institute Canadian Tax Simulator (CANTASIM).

TABLE 26

Decile Distribution of the Personal Income Tax
(per cent)

Year	Lower Income Groups			Middle Income Groups				Upper Income Groups		
	1st	2nd	3rd	4th	5th	6th	7th	8th	9th	10th
1976	.05	.6	2.1	3.7	6.0	9.5	10.3	13.7	17.1	37.3
1978	.03	.3	1.5	4.1	6.5	8.6	11.7	14.7	19.5	33.2

Source: Statistics Canada and Fraser Institute Canadian Tax Simulator (CANTASIM).

the tax distribution in 1978. Whereas up until 1978 there had been a more or less steady increase in the tax burden borne by the upper third of income groups (that is to say, the top three income deciles), during the interval 1976 to 1978, the share of the top group fell markedly. As can be seen from Table 25, during 1976 the top three income deciles accounted for fully 66.5 per cent of the total tax payments. By 1978 this had fallen to 59.6 per cent of the total. Of course, the decline in the tax burden borne by the top three income deciles was matched by a corresponding increase in the tax burden faced by the middle income deciles. For example, the fourth to seventh income deciles which had borne 27.3 per cent of the total tax burden in 1976, by 1978 were bearing 33.5 per cent — an increase of 6.2 percentage points. This almost completely matches the 6.9 percentage point reduction in the tax burden borne by the upper income group.

The reasons for this shift in the tax burden are somewhat difficult to isolate. But at least three separate factors seem to be involved. Tables 26, 27 and 28 help to illuminate the various determining elements. The first of these is the marginal shift in the incidence of the personal income tax system.

As Table 26 shows, there has been a very modest shift in the incidence of the personal income tax system away from the top income deciles and toward the middle income deciles. The top three income groups accounted for only 67.4 per cent of total income tax payments in 1978 down from 68.1 per cent in 1976. This modest shift was accompanied by a dramatic change within the upper three deciles. Whereas in 1976 the highest income decile paid 37.3 per cent of the total personal income tax burden, by 1978 this decile's share had dropped to only 33.2 per cent.

A second and determining factor in the decline in the share of taxes paid by the top three deciles has been the change in the incidence of the capital related taxes in the interval between 1976 and 1978. The 'capital related taxes,' are chiefly property taxes and corporate profit

TABLE 27
Decile Distribution of Profit Taxes and Property Taxes

Profit Taxes

Year	Lower Income Groups			Middle Income Groups				Upper Income Groups		
	1st	2nd	3rd	4th	5th	6th	7th	8th	9th	10th
1976	1.3	3.5	5.5	6.6	4.1	3.3	3.8	10.7	18.1	43.4
1978	1.7	4.6	8.3	9.1	8.5	7.5	8.0	9.2	11.8	31.2

Property Taxes

1976	1.3	3.5	5.5	6.6	4.1	3.3	3.8	10.7	18.1	43.4
1978	1.7	4.7	8.3	9.5	8.6	7.4	8.0	8.9	11.2	31.7

Source: Statistics Canada and Fraser Institute Canadian Tax Simulator (CANTASIM).

TABLE 28
Decile Distribution of Capital Income

Year	Lower Income Groups			Middle Income Groups				Upper Income Groups		
	1st	2nd	3rd	4th	5th	6th	7th	8th	9th	10th
1976	1.3	3.5	5.5	6.6	4.1	3.3	3.8	10.7	18.1	43.4
1978	1.7	4.6	8.3	9.1	8.5	7.5	8.0	9.1	11.8	31.2

Source: Statistics Canada and Fraser Institute Canadian Tax Simulator (CANTASIM).

taxes. As Table 27 shows, the change in the pattern of these taxes has been truly astounding. The effect of the shift is such that in 1978 the top three income deciles paid only 51.8 per cent of the total property tax burden, for example, whereas they had been paying 72.2 per cent of it as late as 1976.

Analysis of the underlying factors reveals that the reason for the dramatic shift in the incidence of the capital taxes has been the change in the distribution of capital income amongst Canadians. The procedure for allocating the burden of capital taxes, such as the Corporate Profits Tax, property taxation, and so on, is to allocate them to individuals on the basis of the individual's receipt of income from capital. (This is done because economic analysis suggests that taxes on capital reduce all capital income.) Between 1976 and 1978 there was a significant change in the distribution of capital income especially between high and middle income earners. The extent of this change can be seen in Table 28 which displays the distribution of total capital income in the two years.

One factor which underlies all of the distribution series is the massive surge in the number of individuals in the upper income classes. In 1976, for example, only 16.9 per cent of the population had an income of $25,000 or more. By 1978, 25.8 per cent of the population enjoyed an income at least as large as that. Much of this increase in the number of families in the higher income groups is a result of the fact that an increasing number of families contains two income earners whose joint income pushes the family into the higher bracket. The implication of this for the distribution of taxation amongst families is that the upper income deciles seem to be paying less and less tax because they are composed increasingly of individuals with lower incomes.

As noted in Chapter 2, two incomes totalling, say, $30,000 are taxed less in total (by the income tax structure) than one income of $30,000. Since upper income families are increasingly composed of two income earners, the

TABLE 29

Decile Distribution of Tax Rates
(per cent)

Year	Lower Income Groups			Middle Income Groups				Upper Income Groups		
	1st	2nd	3rd	4th	5th	6th	7th	8th	9th	10th
1961	19.9	19.9	19.9	20.4	20.9	21.3	23.2	23.3	24.6	32.9
1969	20.6	21.5	25.1	26.4	27.8	27.4	28.2	29.7	30.6	38.2
1972	17.0	18.7	23.8	26.2	28.0	29.6	29.7	31.0	32.2	38.1
1974	21.4	21.5	26.8	27.6	29.7	30.2	30.9	32.5	33.9	39.6
1976	15.7	20.9	25.2	27.4	27.0	27.3	27.9	31.0	33.4	38.8
1978	16.3	22.7	26.4	29.1	29.9	30.0	30.7	31.7	32.8	33.2

Source: Fraser Institute Canadian Tax Simulator (CANTASIM).

average tax rate in this income range has been falling. And, during the latter part of the 1969-1976 period the number of two income earner families included in the top income brackets has increased dramatically.

In 1969, only 27 per cent of the top income families had two income earners: by 1976 this figure had risen to 37 per cent. The upper income group is disproportionately affected by this phenomenon because if two income earners are earning the average national income, their family falls into the highest income group.

There is also, however, some evidence that the rates of taxation have been declining, particularly those experienced by the upper income groups. Thus, for example, in 1976 the top decile of income tax filers in Canada paid an average tax rate of 22.2 per cent. However, by 1978 the average tax rate of the top group had dropped to 19.9 per cent. To some considerable extent this drop in the average tax rate has been due to the increasing extent to which Canadians have taken advantage of the "loopholes" which the government has inserted in the tax system to encourage the development of various sectors of the economy such as oil exploration, rental housing, and Canadian films.

Another feature of developments since 1976 has been the extent to which middle incomes have increased more rapidly than incomes in the upper income groups. For example, between 1976 and 1978 the average income of families in the top income decile increased at only half the rate that was experienced by the average family. This is quite clearly reflected in Table 23 which shows the distribution of income by decile and income group. Whereas, in 1976 nearly 60 per cent of all income earned was earned by the top three income deciles, by 1978 only 56.4 per cent was earned by the upper three income deciles.

Two further implications of the tax distribution for 1978 are interesting to note. The first is that by 1978 the tax system had become virtually flat in this incidence across income groups as is evidenced in Table 29. The top tax rate

TABLE 30

Increase in Tax Rates by Decile since 1961

Lower Income Groups			Middle Income Groups				Upper Income Groups		
1st	2nd	3rd	4th	5th	6th	7th	8th	9th	10th
-3.6	2.8	6.5	8.7	9.0	8.7	7.5	8.4	8.2	.3

Source: Fraser Institute Canadian Tax Simulator (CANTASIM).

on average was 33.2 per cent paid by the tenth income decile, whereas the fourth paid a rate of 29.1 per cent; a very narrow margin of difference. The one remaining group which continues to enjoy a below average system of tax rates is that composed of the three lower income deciles which had, respectively, 16.3, 22.7, and 26.4 per cent tax rates. The reason the tax system has become more like a proportional tax system is evident from Table 30 which shows the increase in the tax rates by deciles since 1961. It is very clearly the case that the brunt of the burden of tax increases since 1961 has been borne by the middle income groups which, on average, have seen their tax rates increase by seven percentage points or more.

WHO PAYS THE TAX BILL?

As can be seen from Table 25, the largest portion of the tax burden ultimately settles on the highest income group. In 1978, the top 10 per cent of Canadian families paid 30 per cent of all taxes paid. The top 30 per cent of families paid about 60 per cent of all taxes paid. Of course, while the tax burden fell disproportionately on the top 30 per cent of families, that group also received a substantial fraction of the income. In 1978, the top 30 per cent earned 56.4 per cent. While this was down noticeably from the 59.5 per cent of the total earned in 1976, it is larger than the 53.6 per cent share this group received in 1961.

In 1978 the top 30 per cent of income earners had an average cash income of $35,706 and included all families whose incomes were above $24,376. (This compares to an average income of $32,615 in 1976 and an entry income of $21,494 in that year.)

THE RAGS-TO-RICHES TAX BURDEN

The notion that a tax system may discourage people from improving their income situation suggests the value of calculating the extent to which Canadians' individual tax situations would have changed during the 1961 to 1980 period if their incomes had increased. Table 31 presents the results of a tax analysis for a hypothetical Canadian individual whose income grew steadily from half the average in 1961 to twice the average in 1980. This "Horatio Alger's" income grew from $2,750 in 1961 to $45,000 in 1980.

In 1961, an income of $2,750 attracted a tax bill of $960, or an average tax rate on total income of 20.1 per cent. By 1972, the hypothetical income earner had income of $13,871 and paid taxes of $6,229, or a tax rate of 29.6 per cent. Finally, in 1980, income was $45,000, taxes paid amounted to $24,271, and the average tax rate on total income had risen to 39.1 per cent. In each case the tax calculation does not include the amount of debt accumulated by government on behalf of the taxpayer. Including debt, the increase in tax burden is even more dramatic, as can be seen in Table 31.

Over the nineteen year period 1961-1980, the hypothetical Horatio experienced a 1,536.4 per cent increase in total income. Over the same period, taxes paid increased by 2,428.2 per cent excluding debt. Including debt they increased 2,849.8 per cent.

Meanwhile, the tax rate faced by the individual increased 66.5 per cent. In improving their circumstances, Canadian Horatio Algers would have earned a total income over the period of $311,578 and paid total taxes of $150,073.

TABLE 31

The Rags-To-Riches Tax Burden

	1961	1965	1969	1972	1974	1976	1978	1980	Percentage Increase 1961-1980
Cash income (assumed)*	$2,750	$4,953	$8,922	$13,871	$18,616	$24,984	$33,530	$45,000	1,536.4%
Total income	4,776	8,465	15,004	23,047	30,684	40,850	54,384	72,403	1,416.0%
Taxes paid (excluding debt)**	960	1,895	3,741	6,229	8,752	12,296	17,275	24,271	2,428.2%
Taxes paid (including debt)**	960	1,957	3,991	6,811	9,726	13,888	19,831	28,318	2,849.8%
Tax rate on total income (excluding debt)***	20.1%	22.4%	24.9%	27.0%	28.5%	30.1%	31.8%	33.5%	66.6%
Tax rate on total income (including debt)***	20.1%	23.1%	26.6%	29.6%	31.7%	34.0%	36.5%	39.1%	94.5%

*Assumed income was arrived at by assuming that income increased smoothly in equal percentage increases from the poverty level in 1961 to high income in 1980.

**Taxes are calculated for 1961, 1969, 1972, 1974, 1976, 1978, and 1980 using the tax tables in the study. The figures are shown in two ways, one including debt and one excluding government debt.

***It was assumed that the tax rate between 1961 and 1969 increased smoothly in equal percentages and that method was used to calculate the 1965 tax rate. The 1965 tax rates were applied to total income in order to calculate the 1965 taxes paid. The taxes paid were also calculated on a pre-debt and post-debt basis.

Chapter 6
Taxes Across Canada

This year for the first time the Fraser Institute is able to provide an analysis of taxation on a province-by-province basis. The Institute's tax simulator has now been loaded with data for all ten provinces and it has been possible to construct tax estimates for individual provinces.

Table 32 presents the tax situation for the average family by province of residence. Average family in this context is taken to mean a family unit which had an average income for the province of residence. Thus, for example, the average family in Newfoundland had an income of $17,500 in 1980 whereas the average family in Ontario had an income of $24,500 and so on. It is very interesting to survey the results for each of these families and to see just how the tax bill varies from province to province and from category to category. It is particularly interesting to see which provinces have the highest propensity to tax in each of the tax categories. In this regard there are some real surprises. The most obvious surprise in the table is that the most heavily taxed family in the country is an Albertan family. The average Albertan family, according to the table, pays a total of $16,000 in tax on an income of only $21,000. This seems astonishing indeed and requires some explanation—particularly in light of the popular notion that Albertans are the least taxed Canadians because of the revenue from the petroleum in that province.

TABLE 32

Taxes of the Average Family by Province, 1980
(dollars)

Prov.	Avg. Cash Income	Full Income	Total Income Before Tax	Profits Tax	Income Tax	Sales Tax	Liquor, Tobacco, Amusement, and Other Excise Taxes	Auto, Fuel, & Motor Vehicle License Taxes	Social Security, Pension, Medical & Hospital Taxes	Property Tax	Natural Resources Taxes	Import Duties	Other Taxes	Total Taxes
Nfld.	17,500	21,535	27,256	439	2,203	1,326	322	416	1,126	185	97	381	224	6,719
PEI	16,000	17,722	22,673	333	1,800	775	318	373	1,067	403	11	409	40	5,529
N.S.	16,500	20,483	27,776	391	2,245	1,092	515	387	1,348	451	18	369	186	7,003
N.B.	16,000	19,142	25,493	515	2,015	1,103	441	361	1,079	629	49	344	103	6,637
P.Q.	22,000	23,302	31,331	585	3,656	1,522	507	511	1,314	587	46	391	875	9,995
Ont.	24,500	26,289	35,140	753	3,486	1,791	440	400	1,720	752	40	394	439	10,214
Man.	18,500	22,898	30,083	778	2,473	905	411	336	1,107	1,038	70	349	369	7,836
Sask.	18,000	22,913	32,038	921	2,373	783	462	368	1,096	949	1,885	401	289	9,527
Alta.	21,000	25,253	40,587	2,758	3,327	462	498	144	1,512	885	5,648	456	336	16,024
B.C.	23,500	24,578	33,513	917	3,263	1,355	406	306	1,386	980	493	381	261	9,749
Canada	22,500	24,666	33,685	886	3,345	1,432	469	399	1,485	749	647	403	491	10,306

Source: Statistics Canada data on taxes and income.

In allocating the tax burden in the Province of Alberta, it became obvious at an early stage of the analysis that there was a problem. The source of the difficulty was that the total amount of tax collected in the Province of Alberta from the petroleum industry totally swamped the other sources of taxation in Alberta and, indeed, in any of the other provinces. In the case of Alberta, our estimates suggest that some $7,254 of natural resource revenues were extracted for each family resident in Alberta in 1980. This was composed of $5,648 in direct natural resource taxes and some $1,606 in estimated corporate profit taxes associated with petroleum development. Of course, these petroleum related taxes are not collected directly from the taxpaying public in Alberta, rather they are collected, indirectly, from the corporations who recover the oil and gas from the ground. It is nevertheless the case, that the gas and oil in the ground in Alberta belongs to the people of Alberta. It is appropriate, therefore, to regard the taxes which are paid as a result of the exploitation of these petroleum resources, as the income of Albertans and, hence, a tax on Albertans.

While this is the appropriate technical treatment of petroleum resource taxes it does confuse somewhat the inter-provincial comparison of tax burdens. Many Canadians, for example, would like nothing better than to live in Alberta and be subject to what looks like the heaviest tax burden in the country. That, of course, is because of the high incomes which are available to those fortunate enough to work in the petroleum industry in Alberta and because of the relatively high level of services provided by government and the low level of direct tax which Albertans are compelled to pay. If we subtract from the $16,024 total tax bill that the average Albertan family faces, the $7,254 per family which was collected on their behalf from the petroleum industry, we find that the total tax bill of Albertans is reduced very significantly to $8,770 for the average family. The implications of this for the gross tax

TABLE 33

Provincial Tax Rates* as a Percentage of Cash Income, Full Income, and Total Income Before Tax, 1980

Province	Cash Income	Full Income	Total Income Before Tax
Newfoundland	38.4	31.2	24.7
Prince Edward Island	34.6	31.2	24.4
Nova Scotia	42.4	34.2	25.2
New Brunswick	41.5	34.7	26.0
Quebec	45.4	42.9	31.9
Ontario	41.7	38.9	29.1
Manitoba	42.4	34.2	26.0
Saskatchewan**	52.9	41.6	29.7
	(44.6)	(35.0)	(25.0)
Alberta**	76.3	63.5	39.5
	(41.8)	(34.7)	(21.6)
British Columbia**	41.5	39.7	29.1
	(39.4)	(37.7)	(27.6)
Canada	45.8	41.8	30.6

Source: Fraser Institute Canadian Tax Simulator (CANTASIM).

*For the average family in 1980 in each of the provinces.

**Bracketed figures are the tax rates resulting when natural resource taxes are removed from the average family's tax bill.

rate faced by Albertans can be seen in Table 33 wherein the bracketed figures represent the tax rate calculated on a basis which excludes the natural resource taxes. Thus, for example, in the case of the tax rate on cash income, the rate is reduced from an unbelievable 76.3 per cent down to 41.8 per cent which is among the lowest in the country.

A similar adjustment for natural resource taxes has been made for both Saskatchewan and British Columbia. Adjusted tax rates are also shown for these provinces in Table 33. As can be seen from that table the fraction of income paid in taxes by the average Canadian family varies very significantly from province to province. Excluding for the moment the unusual case of Alberta, we find that the average rate of taxation on total income before tax varies from a low of 24.4 per cent in Prince Edward Island to a high of 31.9 per cent in Quebec. It is also

interesting to note that the relatively high income provinces of British Columbia, Saskatchewan, and Ontario all
have tax rates in the 29 per cent range — very close to the
national average tax rate.

Once the tax rates have been adjusted for the natural
resource taxes, it is quite clear that Alberta lives up to its
image of being the low tax province with an average tax
rate of 21.6 per cent on total income earned.

As Table 32 reveals, there are also some interesting
variations within the various tax categories — for example,
the relative dependence on property taxation and income
taxation as revenue sources. Outstanding in this regard is
the reliance of Manitoba on property taxation and
Newfoundland's almost complete lack of this form of taxation. In the case of Manitoba, 13.25 cents out of every tax
dollar paid by Manitoba taxpayers is collected in the form
of property taxes. In the case of Newfoundland, only 2.75
cents of the taxpayers' dollar is collected in the form of
property tax. Newfoundland's lack of activity on the property tax front is more than compensated for by sales tax
activity. In fact, Newfoundland has the distinction of being
the province wherein taxpayers pay more sales tax than
any other province in the country. Fully 20 per cent of all
taxes collected in Newfoundland accrue in the form of
sales tax revenues. Of course, this 20 per cent is made up of
both the provincial retail sales tax, which is obvious to
every taxpayer, as well as the federal and provincial sales
taxes which are paid for at the wholesale level and are not
evident to retail customers.

Income tax is most heavily relied upon in Quebec
which collects nearly 37 per cent of its total revenue in that
form. Quebec also had the highest rate of income taxation
in that the average income earner in Quebec faced a 16.6
per cent rate of income tax on his cash income. By comparison, the average Prince Edward Islander faced an income
tax rate of only 11.3 per cent. The average Quebecer also
paid more auto, fuel, and motor vehicle license taxes than
income earners elsewhere in the country — the $511 on

TABLE 34

Decile Distribution of Taxes by Province, 1980
(per cent)

Province	Lower Income Groups			Middle Income Groups				Upper Income Groups		
	1st	2nd	3rd	4th	5th	6th	7th	8th	9th	10th
Newfoundland	.5	1.1	3.3	5.7	7.5	9.3	11.0	14.2	17.2	30.3
Prince Edward Island	.6	1.1	3.0	4.9	6.9	9.2	11.8	13.9	17.9	30.9
Nova Scotia	.6	1.1	3.2	5.0	7.1	8.7	11.4	13.6	19.0	30.3
New Brunswick	.8	1.4	2.8	4.7	6.8	8.9	11.8	13.9	17.7	31.1
Quebec	.4	1.9	3.7	6.3	7.2	8.9	11.5	13.8	17.1	29.3
Ontario	.7	2.5	4.5	6.6	7.8	8.6	10.3	12.5	18.0	28.7
Manitoba	.7	1.2	3.4	5.7	8.3	9.5	10.6	14.0	17.1	29.6
Saskatchewan	1.1	2.0	4.3	5.7	7.0	9.0	11.0	13.0	16.7	30.2
Alberta	1.0	3.5	5.6	6.1	7.6	9.0	10.0	12.6	15.7	29.0
British Columbia	.7	2.1	4.1	6.0	8.0	8.5	10.4	13.3	18.7	28.3
Canada	.7	2.2	4.2	6.2	7.7	8.8	10.8	13.0	16.6	30.0

Source: Fraser Institute Canadian Tax Simulator (CANTASIM).

average paid by Quebec motorists accounted for just over 5 per cent of the total tax bill that Quebecers face.

In comparing these tax results for the various provinces, it is important to remember that the standard of comparison is the average family. That is to say, the family in each province whose income was average. It is, therefore, the case that the individuals in different provinces will have different incomes since the average income in each province varies considerably. And, some of the differences in tax burden between the provinces is due to nothing more than the differences in income.

Table 34 provides a distribution of taxes by province according to population decile. The great benefit of this table is that it is independent of the incomes within each province and makes possible a comparison of the provinces according to how the tax burden is spread within that province amongst the various income groups. The outcome of this analysis as reflected in the table is simply astounding in that there seems to be very little variation amongst the provinces in the extent of the progressivity or regressivity of the tax systems in the various provinces. That is to say, the upper income groups tend to absorb about 60 per cent of the total tax bill with some minor variations around that. In the case of Prince Edward Island, Nova Scotia, and New Brunswick there is a tendency for the tax burden borne by the upper income group to be relatively heavier than in the other provinces and in the case of Alberta, Saskatchewan, and Ontario, some tendency for the tax burden of the upper income groups to be lower than the average.

The stability of the distribution series in each of the provinces is made the more remarkable by the fact that there is such a different reliance on the different forms of taxation in the various provinces. This fact, which was pointed out above in the discussion of Table 32, ought to provide some variation in the tax rates unless, of course, the differences in the progressivity and regressivity of the

TABLE 35

Tax Rates by Decile by Province, 1980
(per cent)

(Income Measure = Total Income Before Tax)

Province	Lower Income Groups			Middle Income Groups				Upper Income Groups		
	1st	2nd	3rd	4th	5th	6th	7th	8th	9th	10th
Newfoundland	7.5	8.4	15.8	21.2	23.1	24.8	25.8	28.0	29.7	32.5
Prince Edward Island	9.1	9.9	13.7	17.9	20.8	24.0	24.6	25.2	26.2	27.4
Nova Scotia	9.7	13.2	18.7	22.1	24.6	25.0	27.3	28.5	29.3	30.7
New Brunswick	12.9	14.9	16.2	21.0	23.8	25.7	27.8	29.0	29.8	30.4
Quebec	7.8	16.8	23.0	29.1	29.1	31.3	33.0	34.1	35.1	35.2
Ontario	17.4	24.5	27.7	29.3	28.9	28.9	29.3	29.9	31.2	31.1
Manitoba	11.5	15.2	18.9	23.5	26.1	26.1	25.6	27.6	28.2	27.9
Saskatchewan*	19.3	24.2	27.3	28.3	28.1	29.4	30.5	30.9	31.8	33.7
	(15.3)	(19.2)	(21.6)	(22.4)	(22.3)	(23.3)	(24.2)	(24.5)	(25.2)	(26.7)
Alberta*	49.3	42.9	42.7	40.7	41.0	39.5	38.6	39.8	41.0	45.6
	(26.7)	(23.2)	(23.1)	(22.1)	(22.2)	(21.4)	(20.9)	(21.6)	(22.2)	(24.7)
British Columbia*	20.6	22.9	26.6	28.7	30.7	29.2	29.0	32.0	31.1	31.6
	(20.0)	(22.2)	(25.8)	(27.9)	(29.8)	(28.4)	(28.2)	(31.1)	(30.2)	(30.7)
Canada	16.7	23.1	26.9	29.5	30.2	30.4	31.0	32.0	33.2	33.5

Source: Fraser Institute Canadian Tax Simulator (CANTASIM).

*Bracketed figures are the tax rates resulting when natural resource taxes are removed from the average family's tax bill.

various tax rates are offsetting. From Table 34 it appears that the various tax measures are offsetting in their effect on the rate of progressivity of the provincial tax systems.

However, as Table 35 shows, there are some important differences between the tax systems in the various provinces. Table 35 highlights these differences in the form of the average tax rates which are payable by the various income deciles in the different provinces. Thus, for example, in Newfoundland the lowest income decile paid a tax rate of 7.5 per cent on average, whereas the top decile paid a tax rate of 32.5 per cent. In Quebec, on the other hand, the top decile paid 35.2 per cent, whereas the bottom decile paid 7.8 per cent.

Like the other tables, the tax rate table is dominated by the effects of the natural resource taxes in the Western provinces. The numbers in parentheses are the tax rates for these provinces adjusted to remove the effect of natural resource taxation. Once the effects of these have been removed the pattern of tax rates in the Western provinces is seen to conform more closely to the national average figures.

Appendix

HOW TO USE THE INCOME TABLES

Tables A-1 to A-11 are the 1980 Income Tables for each of the ten provinces and Canada as a whole. You will be able to locate within $500 your cash income in the first column of each Income Table. You will then be able to establish for the province in which you reside, your full cash income, income from government, hidden income, hidden purchasing power loss, and total income before tax.

Step 1.   Make a rough calculation of your family's cash income from all sources for the year 1980.

			$
	eg. *Alberta*		
Example:	Husband's income in 1980	=	10,500
	Wife's income in 1980	=	10,500
	Dependent daughter's income in 1980	=	200
	Total cash income	=	21,200

Step 2.   Since the table is only calculated to the nearest $500, round off your cash income to the nearest $500.

    Example: $21,200

         Round to nearest $500   = $21,000

Step 3.   If your income exceeded $45,000, skip to Step 5. If not, proceed through Steps 3 and 4.

    Locate the line in the 1980 Income Table for your province of residence that has the entry $21,000 in the first column. (The column headed "Your Cash Income".)

    Example: See the line in the 1980 Income Table.

Step 4.   Read off Full Cash Income, Income from Government, Hidden Income, Hidden Purchasing Power Loss, and Total Income Before Tax.

Example:

Your Cash Income	Full Cash Income	Income from Gov't	Hidden Income	Hidden Purchasing Power Loss	Total Income Before Tax
$	$	$	$	$	$
21,000	25,253	1,819	3,045	12,289	40,587

Step 5.   If your cash income exceeded $45,000 you will have to use the Detailed Income Calculation Schedules which accompany each Income Table.

TABLE A-1

1980 Income Table for the Province of Alberta

Your Cash Income	Your Full Cash Income	Income from Government	Hidden Income	Hidden Purchasing Power Loss	Total Income Before Tax
		(Dollars per family)			
5000	7247	4365	961	4482	12690
5500	8339	4681	1180	5305	14824
6000	8817	4589	1532	6370	16718
6500	9294	4498	1884	7434	18612
7000	9982	4525	1837	8196	20015
7500	10676	4555	1778	8949	21403
8000	11370	4585	1720	9702	22792
8500	11930	4452	1684	9948	23562
9000	12305	4093	1679	9492	23477
9500	12680	3734	1675	9037	23393
10000	13055	3375	1671	8582	23308
10500	13430	3016	1666	8127	23223
11000	13862	2813	1773	8188	23823
11500	14320	2683	1931	8491	24741
12000	14777	2552	2089	8793	25659
12500	15235	2421	2247	9095	26577
13000	15693	2291	2405	9397	27495
13500	16235	2216	2382	9601	28218
14000	16782	2144	2348	9799	28929
14500	17330	2073	2314	9996	29640
15000	17877	2001	2280	10194	30351
15500	18424	1930	2247	10392	31062
16000	18973	1860	2216	10589	31778
16500	19607	1855	2300	10765	32673
17000	20241	1851	2385	10941	33567
17500	20876	1847	2470	11116	34462
18000	21510	1842	2554	11292	35356
18500	22144	1838	2639	11468	36251
19000	22778	1834	2724	11644	37145
19500	23412	1829	2808	11819	38040
20000	24046	1825	2893	11995	38934
20500	24680	1821	2978	12171	39829
21000	25253	1819	3045	12289	40587
21500	25776	1821	3097	12360	41232
22000	26299	1822	3149	12430	41878
22500	26822	1823	3201	12501	42524
23000	27345	1824	3253	12572	43169
23500	27867	1825	3305	12642	43815
24000	28390	1826	3357	12713	44460
24500	28913	1828	3409	12784	45106
25000	29436	1829	3461	12854	45752

TABLE A-1 continued

Your Cash Income	Your Full Cash Income	Income from Government	Hidden Income	Hidden Purchasing Power Loss	Total Income Before Tax
		(Dollars per family)			
25500	29959	1830	3513	12925	46397
26000	30482	1831	3565	12996	47043
26500	31005	1832	3618	13066	47688
27000	31561	1829	3781	13394	48736
27500	32130	1824	3991	13830	49951
28000	32700	1819	4201	14265	51166
28500	33270	1815	4411	14700	52381
29000	33839	1810	4621	15135	53596
29500	34409	1805	4831	15570	54811
30000	34979	1800	5041	16006	56025
30500	35549	1795	5251	16441	57240
31000	36118	1790	5461	16876	58455
31500	36688	1785	5671	17311	59670
32000	37258	1781	5881	17746	60885
32500	37828	1776	6091	18181	62100
33000	38406	1780	6205	18468	63080
33500	38986	1785	6305	18731	64022
34000	39566	1791	6405	18994	64965
34500	40146	1796	6504	19257	65907
35000	40726	1802	6604	19520	66850
35500	41305	1807	6703	19783	67792
36000	41885	1813	6803	20046	68735
36500	42465	1818	6903	20309	69677
37000	43045	1824	7002	20572	70620
37500	43625	1829	7102	20835	71562
38000	44205	1835	7202	21099	72505
38500	44784	1840	7302	21367	73453
39000	45348	1838	7440	21878	74666
39500	45913	1836	7578	22389	75880
40000	46477	1834	7716	22900	77093
40500	47041	1832	7854	23412	78307
41000	47606	1830	7992	23923	79520
41500	48170	1828	8130	24434	80734
42000	48734	1826	8267	24946	81947
42500	49298	1824	8405	25457	83161
43000	49863	1822	8543	25968	84374
43500	50427	1820	8681	26480	85588
44000	50991	1818	8819	26991	86801
44500	51556	1816	8957	27502	88015
45000	52120	1814	9095	28013	89228

SCHEDULE A-1

1980 Detailed Income Calculation for the Province of Alberta

Your Cash Income

1. Full Cash Income	= Cash Income x 1.158	= _____
2. Of which Income from Government	= $1,814	= _____
3. Hidden Income	= Cash Income x .202	= $ 1,814
4. Hidden Purchasing Power Loss	= Cash Income x .623	= _____
Total Income before Tax	= 1 + 3 + 4	= _____

EXAMPLE:

Your Cash Income

1. Full Cash Income	= $70,000 x 1.158	= $ 70,000
2. Of which Income from Government	= $1,814	= $ 81,060
3. Hidden Income	= $70,000 x .202	= $ 1,814
4. Hidden Purchasing Power Loss	= $70,000 x .623	= $ 14,140
Total Income before Tax	= $81,060 + $14,140 + $43,610	= $ 43,610
		= $138,810

Appendix

TABLE A-2

1980 Income Table for the Province of British Columbia

Your Cash Income	Your Full Cash Income	Income from Government	Hidden Income	Hidden Purchasing Power Loss	Total Income Before Tax
		(Dollars per family)			
5000	6219	4168	468	1091	7779
5500	7166	4557	518	1205	8890
6000	7698	4111	862	1467	10027
6500	8217	3636	1216	1733	11166
7000	8722	3653	1365	2055	12142
7500	9215	4134	1320	2429	12965
8000	9708	4615	1276	2803	13787
8500	10201	5097	1232	3177	14610
9000	10694	5183	1260	3300	15254
9500	11187	5193	1302	3375	15864
10000	11681	5202	1344	3449	16474
10500	12174	5212	1386	3524	17084
11000	12667	5221	1429	3598	17694
11500	13127	4964	1696	3715	18538
12000	13584	4688	1979	3836	19399
12500	14042	4412	2262	3956	20260
13000	14499	4136	2546	4076	21121
13500	14957	3866	2817	4201	21975
14000	15429	3805	2683	4484	22596
14500	15901	3743	2549	4767	23217
15000	16373	3682	2416	5050	23838
15500	16845	3620	2282	5333	24459
16000	17317	3559	2148	5616	25080
16500	17789	3497	2014	5899	25702
17000	18281	3341	2048	5913	26241
17500	18775	3174	2100	5897	26772
18000	19269	3007	2152	5882	27303
18500	19763	2841	2205	5866	27834
19000	20257	2674	2257	5850	28365
19500	20752	2507	2309	5834	28895
20000	21246	2340	2362	5819	29426
20500	21740	2173	2414	5803	29957
21000	22234	2007	2466	5787	30488
21500	22726	1857	2523	5778	31027
22000	23189	1878	2622	5838	31648
22500	23652	1899	2721	5898	32270
23000	24115	1919	2820	5957	32892
23500	24578	1940	2918	6017	33513
24000	25041	1961	3017	6076	34135
24500	25504	1982	3116	6136	34756
25000	25967	2003	3215	6195	35378

TABLE A-2 continued

1980 Income Table for the Province of British Columbia

Your Cash Income	Your Full Cash Income	Income from Government	Hidden Income	Hidden Purchasing Power Loss	Total Income Before Tax
		(Dollars per family)			
25500	26430	2023	3314	6255	35999
26000	26893	2044	3413	6315	36621
26500	27356	2065	3512	6374	37242
27000	27819	2086	3611	6434	37864
27500	28283	2107	3710	6493	38485
28000	28678	2110	3757	6656	39090
28500	29059	2111	3793	6838	39691
29000	29440	2112	3830	7021	40291
29500	29822	2112	3866	7204	40892
30000	30203	2113	3903	7387	41493
30500	30585	2113	3939	7570	42094
31000	30966	2114	3976	7753	42695
31500	31347	2114	4012	7936	43295
32000	31729	2115	4049	8119	43896
32500	32110	2116	4086	8301	44497
33000	32492	2116	4122	8484	45098
33500	32873	2117	4159	8667	45699
34000	33385	2089	4264	8769	46418
34500	33995	2039	4420	8811	47226
35000	34605	1990	4576	8854	48034
35500	35214	1941	4732	8896	48842
36000	35824	1891	4888	8938	49650
36500	36434	1842	5044	8980	50458
37000	37043	1793	5200	9022	51266
37500	37653	1743	5357	9064	52074
38000	38263	1694	5513	9106	52882
38500	38873	1644	5669	9148	53690
39000	39482	1595	5825	9190	54498
39500	40092	1546	5981	9232	55306
40000	40691	1520	6168	9333	56192
40500	41267	1544	6421	9562	57250
41000	41842	1569	6675	9791	58308
41500	42418	1593	6929	10020	59367
42000	42994	1618	7182	10249	60425
42500	43569	1642	7436	10478	61483
43000	44145	1667	7690	10707	62541
43500	44721	1691	7943	10936	63599
44000	45296	1716	8197	11164	64658
44500	45872	1740	8451	11393	65716
45000	46448	1765	8704	11622	66774

SCHEDULE A-2

1980 Detailed Income Calculation for the Province of British Columbia

Your Cash Income

1. Full Cash Income	= Cash Income x 1.032	= _____
2. Of which Income from Government	= $1,765	= _____
3. Hidden Income	= Cash Income x .193	= $ 1,765
4. Hidden Purchasing Power Loss	= Cash Income x .258	= _____
Total Income before Tax	= 1 + 3 + 4	= _____
		= _____

EXAMPLE:

Your Cash Income

1. Full Cash Income	= $70,000 x 1.032	= $ 70,000
2. Of which Income from Government	= $1,765	= $ 72,240
3. Hidden Income	= $70,000 x .193	= $ 1,765
4. Hidden Purchasing Power Loss	= $70,000 x .258	= $ 13,510
Total Income before Tax	= $72,240 + $13,510 + $18,060	= $ 18,060
		= $103,810

TABLE A-3

1980 Income Table for the Province of Manitoba

Your Cash Income	Your Full Cash Income	Income from Government	Hidden Income	Hidden Purchasing Power Loss	Total Income Before Tax
		(Dollars per family)			
5000	7290	3354	828	1798	9916
5500	8146	3474	988	2111	11245
6000	9035	4140	1228	2242	12504
6500	9924	4807	1467	2372	13763
7000	10574	4864	1479	2447	14501
7500	11093	4585	1365	2492	14950
8000	11613	4306	1252	2536	15400
8500	12132	4027	1138	2580	15850
9000	12717	3820	1241	2877	16835
9500	13301	3613	1343	3174	17819
10000	13886	3406	1446	3471	18803
10500	14471	3199	1549	3768	19788
11000	15062	3009	1650	4046	20758
11500	15686	2913	1745	4210	21641
12000	16311	2818	1840	4374	22525
12500	16936	2723	1935	4538	23409
13000	17560	2627	2030	4701	24292
13500	18123	2537	2092	4821	25037
14000	18533	2460	2073	4832	25438
14500	18943	2384	2053	4843	25839
15000	19354	2307	2033	4854	26241
15500	19764	2230	2013	4865	26642
16000	20174	2153	1993	4876	27043
16500	20618	2086	1988	4890	27497
17000	21188	2056	2040	4916	28144
17500	21758	2025	2091	4941	28790
18000	22328	1995	2143	4966	29436
18500	22898	1965	2195	4991	30083
19000	23467	1934	2246	5016	30729
19500	24037	1904	2298	5041	31376
20000	24607	1873	2349	5066	32022
20500	25177	1843	2401	5091	32669
21000	25746	1813	2453	5116	33315
21500	26326	1796	2516	5217	34059
22000	26915	1793	2591	5393	34898
22500	27504	1790	2666	5568	35738
23000	28093	1787	2741	5744	36577
23500	28682	1785	2816	5919	37417
24000	29271	1782	2890	6095	38256
24500	29860	1779	2965	6270	39096
25000	30449	1776	3040	6446	39936

Appendix

TABLE A-3 continued

1980 Income Table for the Province of Manitoba

Your Cash Income	Your Full Cash Income	Income from Government	Hidden Income	Hidden Purchasing Power Loss	Total Income Before Tax
		(Dollars per family)			
25500	31038	1773	3115	6622	40775
26000	31627	1771	3190	6797	41615
26500	32216	1768	3265	6973	42454
27000	32805	1765	3340	7148	43293
27500	33381	1766	3430	7289	44100
28000	33932	1773	3548	7367	44847
28500	34484	1780	3665	7445	45594
29000	35035	1788	3783	7523	46341
29500	35586	1795	3900	7601	47088
30000	36138	1802	4018	7679	47835
30500	36689	1809	4135	7757	48582
31000	37241	1817	4253	7835	49329
31500	37792	1824	4370	7913	50076
32000	38344	1831	4488	7991	50823
32500	38895	1838	4605	8069	51570
33000	39446	1846	4723	8147	52317
33500	40017	1857	4920	8253	53190
34000	40654	1885	5400	8459	54514
34500	41292	1913	5881	8665	55838
35000	41929	1941	6361	8871	57162
35500	42567	1969	6841	9078	58486
36000	43205	1997	7322	9284	59810
36500	43842	2024	7802	9490	61134
37000	44480	2052	8282	9696	62458
37500	45118	2080	8762	9902	63782
38000	45755	2108	9243	10108	65106
38500	46393	2136	9723	10314	66429
39000	47030	2164	10203	10520	67753
39500	47672	2189	10664	10722	69058
40000	48366	2189	10884	10878	70127
40500	49059	2189	11104	11034	71196
41000	49752	2189	11324	11190	72265
41500	50446	2188	11543	11346	73335
42000	51139	2188	11763	11502	74404
42500	51832	2188	11983	11658	75473
43000	52526	2188	12203	11814	76543
43500	53219	2187	12423	11970	77612
44000	53912	2187	12643	12126	78681
44500	54606	2187	12863	12282	79750
45000	55299	2187	13083	12438	80820

SCHEDULE A-3

1980 Detailed Income Calculation for the Province of Manitoba

Your Cash Income

1. Full Cash Income	= Cash Income x 1.229	=	
2. Of which Income from Government	= $2,187	=	$ 2,187
3. Hidden Income	= Cash Income x .291	=	
4. Hidden Purchasing Power Loss	= Cash Income x .276	=	
Total Income before Tax	= 1 + 3 + 4	=	

EXAMPLE:

Your Cash Income

1. Full Cash Income	= $70,000 x 1.229	=	$ 70,000
2. Of which Income from Government	= $2,187	=	$ 86,030
3. Hidden Income	= $70,000 x .291	=	$ 2,187
4. Hidden Purchasing Power Loss	= $70,000 x .276	=	$ 20,370
Total Income before Tax	= $86,030 + $20,370 + $19,320	=	$ 19,320
		=	$125,720

TABLE A-4

1980 Income Table for the Province of New Brunswick

Your Cash Income	Your Full Cash Income	Income from Government	Hidden Income	Hidden Purchasing Power Loss	Total Income Before Tax
		(Dollars per family)			
5000	6672	4318	357	1244	8272
5500	7373	4864	398	1304	9075
6000	8065	5466	442	1331	9839
6500	8756	5718	523	1436	10714
7000	9445	5603	641	1622	11708
7500	10134	5487	760	1808	12702
8000	10801	5369	877	1996	13674
8500	11209	5213	979	2198	14386
9000	11617	5057	1081	2400	15097
9500	12024	4901	1183	2601	15808
10000	12432	4745	1285	2803	16520
10500	12904	4669	1341	2932	17178
11000	13436	4664	1358	2994	17788
11500	13968	4659	1374	3056	18398
12000	14500	4655	1390	3118	19008
12500	15031	4650	1406	3180	19618
13000	15652	4529	1475	3374	20501
13500	16274	4406	1546	3571	21391
14000	16897	4282	1616	3769	22282
14500	17519	4159	1687	3966	23172
15000	18141	4035	1758	4164	24063
15500	18709	3934	1827	4339	24875
16000	19142	3888	1893	4459	25493
16500	19574	3842	1959	4579	26112
17000	20007	3796	2025	4699	26730
17500	20440	3750	2090	4819	27349
18000	20872	3704	2156	4939	27967
18500	21305	3658	2222	5059	28586
19000	21738	3612	2288	5179	29205
19500	22170	3566	2354	5299	29823
20000	22617	3522	2419	5423	30458
20500	23122	3485	2476	5564	31162
21000	23628	3448	2534	5705	31867
21500	24133	3410	2592	5847	32572
22000	24639	3373	2649	5988	33276
22500	25144	3336	2707	6129	33981
23000	25650	3299	2765	6271	34685
23500	26156	3262	2822	6412	35390
24000	26661	3224	2880	6553	36094
24500	27167	3187	2938	6695	36799
25000	27672	3150	2995	6836	37504

TABLE A-4 continued

1980 Income Table for the Province of New Brunswick

Your Cash Income	Your Full Cash Income	Income from Government	Hidden Income	Hidden Purchasing Power Loss	Total Income Before Tax
		(Dollars per family)			
25500	28178	3113	3053	6977	38208
26000	28770	3149	3186	7108	39064
26500	29383	3202	3337	7236	39955
27000	29995	3255	3487	7364	40846
27500	30608	3309	3637	7492	41737
28000	31220	3362	3788	7621	42628
28500	31833	3415	3938	7749	43519
29000	32445	3468	4089	7877	44410
29500	33057	3521	4239	8005	45301
30000	33670	3574	4389	8133	46192
30500	34282	3628	4540	8261	47083
31000	34895	3681	4690	8389	47974
31500	35488	3703	4867	8587	48942
32000	36058	3685	5078	8873	50009
32500	36627	3668	5289	9159	51075
33000	37197	3650	5500	9444	52141
33500	37766	3633	5711	9730	53207
34000	38335	3615	5922	10016	54273
34500	38905	3598	6133	10302	55340
35000	39474	3580	6344	10588	56406
35500	40043	3562	6555	10874	57472
36000	40613	3545	6766	11160	58538
36500	41182	3527	6977	11446	59605
37000	41752	3511	7193	11722	60667
37500	42327	3518	7484	11856	61667
38000	42902	3525	7776	11991	62668
38500	43476	3531	8067	12126	63669
39000	44051	3538	8358	12260	64670
39500	44626	3545	8650	12395	65671
40000	45201	3551	8941	12529	66671
40500	45776	3558	9233	12664	67672
41000	46351	3565	9524	12798	68673
41500	46926	3571	9815	12933	69674
42000	47501	3578	10107	13067	70675
42500	48076	3585	10398	13202	71676
43000	48650	3591	10689	13337	72676
43500	49225	3598	10981	13471	73677
44000	49800	3604	11272	13606	74678
44500	50375	3611	11564	13740	75679
45000	50950	3618	11855	13875	76680

SCHEDULE A-4

1980 Detailed Income Calculation for the Province of New Brunswick

Your Cash Income

1. Full Cash Income	= Cash Income x 1.132	= _____
2. Of which Income from Government	= $3,618	= $ 3,618
3. Hidden Income	= Cash Income x .263	= _____
4. Hidden Purchasing Power Loss	= Cash Income x .308	= _____
Total Income before Tax	= 1 + 3 + 4	= _____

EXAMPLE:

Your Cash Income

1. Full Cash Income	$70,000 x 1.132	= $ 70,000
2. Of which Income from Government	= $3,618	= $ 79,240
3. Hidden Income	= $70,000 x .263	= $ 3,618
4. Hidden Purchasing Power Loss	= $70,000 x .308	= $ 18,410
		= $ 21,560
Total Income before Tax	= $79,240 + $18,410 + $21,560	= $119,210

TABLE A-5

1980 Income Table for the Province of Newfoundland

Your Cash Income	Your Full Cash Income	Income from Government	Hidden Income	Hidden Purchasing Power Loss	Total Income Before Tax
		(Dollars per family)			
5000	8481	6943	402	538	9421
5500	9418	7668	444	618	10480
6000	10126	8172	374	814	11314
6500	10833	8676	304	1010	12147
7000	11335	8556	380	1319	13034
7500	11792	8300	487	1654	13933
8000	12249	8045	594	1988	14832
8500	12725	7829	686	2289	15700
9000	13265	7746	723	2476	16464
9500	13804	7663	761	2664	17228
10000	14343	7580	798	2851	17992
10500	14882	7498	836	3039	18757
11000	15423	7413	891	3178	19492
11500	15966	7325	969	3255	20190
12000	16509	7238	1047	3333	20888
12500	17051	7150	1125	3410	21587
13000	17594	7062	1203	3488	22285
13500	18060	6981	1242	3577	22880
14000	18484	6901	1260	3674	23418
14500	18907	6821	1278	3770	23955
15000	19331	6742	1296	3866	24493
15500	19754	6662	1314	3963	25031
16000	20177	6583	1332	4059	25569
16500	20622	6570	1358	4144	26125
17000	21079	6591	1388	4223	26690
17500	21536	6612	1418	4303	27256
18000	21992	6634	1447	4382	27821
18500	22449	6655	1477	4461	28387
19000	22905	6676	1507	4540	28952
19500	23362	6698	1537	4620	29518
20000	23818	6719	1567	4699	30084
20500	24275	6740	1596	4778	30649
21000	24734	6755	1628	4864	31226
21500	25234	6679	1687	5033	31954
22000	25735	6603	1745	5203	32682
22500	26235	6526	1803	5372	33410
23000	26735	6450	1862	5541	34138
23500	27235	6374	1920	5711	34866
24000	27735	6298	1979	5880	35594
24500	28235	6222	2037	6049	36322
25000	28736	6146	2096	6219	37050

TABLE A-5 continued

1980 Income Table for the Province of Newfoundland

Your Cash Income	Your Full Cash Income	Income from Government	Hidden Income	Hidden Purchasing Power Loss	Total Income Before Tax
		(Dollars per family)			
25500	29236	6070	2154	6388	37778
26000	29736	5994	2212	6557	38506
26500	30236	5918	2271	6727	39234
27000	30729	5844	2331	6893	39953
27500	31151	5785	2409	7030	40590
28000	31573	5727	2488	7166	41226
28500	31994	5669	2566	7303	41863
29000	32416	5610	2644	7439	42500
29500	32838	5552	2723	7576	43136
30000	33259	5494	2801	7712	43773
30500	33681	5435	2879	7849	44409
31000	34103	5377	2958	7986	45046
31500	34525	5318	3036	8122	45683
32000	34946	5260	3114	8259	46319
32500	35368	5202	3193	8395	46956
33000	35801	5150	3274	8547	47621
33500	36319	5155	3377	8819	48515
34000	36837	5160	3481	9092	49410
34500	37355	5164	3585	9364	50304
35000	37873	5169	3688	9636	51198
35500	38392	5173	3792	9909	52092
36000	38910	5178	3896	10181	52986
36500	39428	5183	3999	10453	53881
37000	39946	5187	4103	10726	54775
37500	40464	5192	4207	10998	55669
38000	40983	5197	4310	11270	56563
38500	41501	5201	4414	11543	57457
39000	42026	5213	4544	11805	58375
39500	42595	5275	4850	11998	59443
40000	43165	5337	5156	12191	60512
40500	43734	5399	5462	12385	61581
41000	44304	5461	5767	12578	62649
41500	44873	5523	6073	12771	63718
42000	45443	5585	6379	12965	64787
42500	46012	5647	6685	13158	65855
43000	46582	5709	6991	13351	66924
43500	47152	5771	7296	13545	67993
44000	47721	5833	7602	13738	69061
44500	48291	5895	7908	13931	70130
45000	48860	5957	8214	14125	71199

SCHEDULE A-5

1980 Detailed Income Calculation for the Province of Newfoundland

Your Cash Income

1. Full Cash Income = Cash Income x 1.086 = _____

2. Of which Income from Government = $5,957 = $ 5,957

3. Hidden Income = Cash Income x .183 = _____

4. Hidden Purchasing Power Loss = Cash Income x .314 = _____

Total Income before Tax = 1 + 3 + 4 = _____

EXAMPLE:

Your Cash Income

1. Full Cash Income = $70,000 x 1.086 = $ 70,000

2. Of which Income from Government = $5,957 = $ 76,020

3. Hidden Income = $70,000 x .183 = $ 5,957

4. Hidden Purchasing Power Loss = $70,000 x .314 = $ 12,810

Total Income before Tax = $76,020 + $12,810 + $21,980 = $110,810

Appendix

TABLE A-6

1980 Income Table for the Province of Nova Scotia

Your Cash Income	Your Full Cash Income	Income from Government	Hidden Income	Hidden Purchasing Power Loss	Total Income Before Tax
		(Dollars per family)			
5000	6727	4712	700	1201	8597
5500	7432	5138	752	1399	9583
6000	8076	5407	651	1597	10324
6500	8720	5675	550	1795	11065
7000	9389	5678	672	1971	12032
7500	10067	5584	877	2139	13082
8000	10744	5490	1081	2306	14132
8500	11404	5382	1269	2477	15150
9000	11928	5166	1328	2668	15924
9500	12452	4950	1387	2860	16698
10000	12976	4733	1446	3051	17472
10500	13499	4517	1505	3242	18246
11000	14057	4303	1603	3427	19087
11500	14698	4095	1797	3595	20090
12000	15339	3886	1991	3764	21093
12500	15980	3677	2185	3932	22097
13000	16620	3469	2379	4100	23100
13500	17216	3352	2507	4210	23933
14000	17760	3342	2559	4252	24571
14500	18304	3332	2612	4294	25210
15000	18848	3322	2664	4336	25849
15500	19392	3311	2716	4379	26487
16000	19937	3301	2768	4421	27126
16500	20483	3293	2785	4507	27775
17000	21032	3287	2756	4651	28439
17500	21582	3280	2726	4794	29102
18000	22131	3274	2697	4938	29766
18500	22680	3268	2668	5081	30429
19000	23230	3262	2638	5225	31093
19500	23779	3256	2609	5369	31757
20000	24329	3250	2580	5512	32420
20500	24878	3244	2550	5656	33084
21000	25427	3237	2521	5799	33747
21500	25959	3211	2645	5949	34553
22000	26487	3179	2811	6100	35397
22500	27014	3147	2976	6251	36242
23000	27541	3115	3142	6403	37086
23500	28069	3083	3308	6554	37930
24000	28596	3051	3474	6705	38775
24500	29123	3019	3639	6856	39619
25000	29651	2987	3805	7008	40463

TABLE A-6 continued

1980 Income Table for the Province of Nova Scotia

Your Cash Income	Your Full Cash Income	Income from Government	Hidden Income	Hidden Purchasing Power Loss	Total Income Before Tax
		(Dollars per family)			
25500	30178	2955	3971	7159	41308
26000	30705	2923	4137	7310	42152
26500	31233	2891	4302	7461	42996
27000	31760	2858	4468	7612	43840
27500	32485	2875	4880	7885	45251
28000	33286	2909	5384	8205	46874
28500	34087	2943	5888	8524	48498
29000	34887	2978	6392	8843	50122
29500	35688	3012	6896	9162	51746
30000	36488	3047	7401	9481	53370
30500	37289	3081	7905	9800	54993
31000	38089	3116	8409	10119	56617
31500	38890	3150	8913	10438	58241
32000	39690	3184	9417	10757	59865
32500	40491	3219	9922	11076	61489
33000	41291	3253	10426	11395	63112
33500	41800	3235	10463	11508	63771
34000	42161	3191	10266	11517	63944
34500	42522	3147	10069	11526	64117
35000	42883	3103	9872	11535	64290
35500	43244	3059	9674	11544	64463
36000	43605	3015	9477	11553	64636
36500	43966	2971	9280	11562	64808
37000	44328	2927	9082	11571	64981
37500	44689	2882	8885	11580	65154
38000	45050	2838	8688	11589	65327
38500	45411	2794	8491	11598	65500
39000	45772	2750	8293	11607	65672
39500	46277	2750	8332	11697	66306
40000	46876	2777	8526	11840	67241
40500	47475	2805	8720	11982	68177
41000	48074	2833	8913	12125	69112
41500	48673	2861	9107	12268	70047
42000	49272	2889	9300	12411	70983
42500	49871	2917	9494	12553	71918
43000	50470	2945	9688	12696	72853
43500	51069	2972	9881	12839	73789
44000	51668	3000	10075	12982	74724
44500	52267	3028	10269	13124	75659
45000	52865	3056	10462	13267	76595

SCHEDULE A-6

1980 Detailed Income Calculation for the Province of Nova Scotia

Your Cash Income

1. Full Cash Income = Cash Income x 1.175 =

2. Of which Income from Government = $3,056 =

3. Hidden Income = Cash Income x .233 = $ 3,056

4. Hidden Purchasing Power Loss = Cash Income x .295 =

Total Income before Tax = 1 + 3 + 4 =

EXAMPLE:

Your Cash Income

1. Full Cash Income = $70,000 x 1.175 = $ 70,000

2. Of which Income from Government = $3,056 = $ 82,250

3. Hidden Income = $70,000 x .233 = $ 3,056

4. Hidden Purchasing Power Loss = $70,000 x .295 = $ 16,310

Total Income before Tax = $82,250 + $16,310 + $20,650 = $ 20,650

= $119,210

TABLE A-7

1980 Income Table for the Province of Ontario

Your Cash Income	Your Full Cash Income	Income from Government	Hidden Income	Hidden Purchasing Power Loss	Total Income Before Tax
		(Dollars per family)			
5000	6369	3880	641	1258	8269
5500	7101	4213	737	1435	9274
6000	7697	4247	859	1546	10103
6500	8294	4281	981	1657	10932
6500	8857	4352	1020	1828	11704
7500	9397	4448	1002	2040	12439
8000	9937	4543	985	2252	13174
8500	10477	4639	968	2464	13909
9000	11131	4529	1138	2768	15038
9500	11793	4406	1320	3077	16191
10000	12455	4282	1503	3387	17344
10500	13117	4159	1685	3696	18498
11000	13758	4029	1866	3988	19613
11500	14115	3805	2032	4048	20195
12000	14471	3580	2199	4108	20778
12500	14828	3355	2365	4168	21361
13000	15184	3131	2531	4228	21944
13500	15574	2951	2653	4306	22533
14000	16103	2955	2588	4458	23149
14500	16632	2960	2523	4611	23766
15000	17161	2965	2459	4763	24382
15500	17690	2969	2394	4915	24999
16000	18219	2974	2329	5067	25615
16500	18739	2967	2273	5207	26218
17000	19177	2860	2291	5235	26703
17500	19615	2753	2309	5264	27187
18000	20053	2646	2327	5292	27672
18500	20491	2539	2345	5321	28156
19000	20929	2432	2363	5349	28641
19500	21366	2324	2381	5378	29126
20000	21804	2217	2399	5406	29610
20500	22242	2110	2418	5435	30095
21000	22680	2003	2436	5463	30579
21500	23149	1936	2467	5513	31129
22000	23672	1944	2524	5601	31798
22500	24195	1951	2581	5690	32466
23000	24719	1959	2638	5778	33135
23500	25242	1967	2695	5867	33803
24000	25766	1974	2751	5955	34472
24500	26289	1982	2808	6043	35140
25000	26812	1989	2865	6132	35809

Appendix

TABLE A-7 continued

Your Cash Income	Your Full Cash Income	Income from Government	Hidden Income	Hidden Purchasing Power Loss	Total Income Before Tax
		(Dollars per family)			
25500	27336	1997	2922	6220	36478
26000	27859	2004	2979	6309	37146
26500	28382	2012	3035	6397	37815
27000	28906	2020	3092	6485	38483
27500	29423	2022	3160	6576	39160
28000	29912	1998	3284	6681	39876
28500	30400	1975	3407	6786	40593
29000	30888	1951	3531	6890	41309
29500	31377	1928	3654	6995	42026
30000	31865	1904	3778	7099	42742
30500	32353	1881	3901	7204	43458
31000	32842	1857	4024	7308	44175
31500	33330	1834	4148	7413	44891
32000	33818	1810	4271	7518	45607
32500	34307	1786	4395	7622	46324
33000	34795	1763	4518	7727	47040
33500	35283	1739	4642	7831	47756
34000	35863	1744	4780	8025	48668
34500	36445	1749	4919	8219	49584
35000	37026	1754	5058	8414	50499
35500	37608	1759	5197	8609	51414
36000	38189	1764	5336	8803	52329
36500	38771	1769	5475	8998	53245
37000	39352	1774	5614	9193	54160
37500	39934	1779	5753	9388	55075
38000	40516	1784	5892	9582	55990
38500	41097	1789	6031	9777	56906
39000	41679	1794	6170	9972	57821
39500	42260	1799	6309	10167	58736
40000	42892	1806	6561	10389	59842
40500	43536	1814	6840	10618	60995
41000	44181	1822	7120	10848	62148
41500	44825	1830	7399	11077	63302
42000	45469	1838	7679	11306	64455
42500	46114	1846	7959	11536	65608
43000	46758	1853	8238	11765	66761
43500	47403	1861	8518	11995	67915
44000	48047	1869	8797	12224	69068
44500	48691	1877	9077	12453	70221
45000	49336	1885	9356	12683	71375

SCHEDULE A-7

1980 Detailed Income Calculation for the Province of Ontario

Your Cash Income =

1. Full Cash Income = Cash Income x 1.096

2. Of which Income from Government = $1,885

3. Hidden Income = Cash Income x .208

4. Hidden Purchasing Power Loss = Cash Income x .282

Total Income before Tax = 1 + 3 + 4

EXAMPLE:

Your Cash Income = $ 70,000

1. Full Cash Income = $70,000 x 1.096 = $ 76,720

2. Of which Income from Government = $1,885 = $ 1,885

3. Hidden Income = $70,000 x .208 = $ 14,560

4. Hidden Purchasing Power Loss = $70,000 x .282 = $ 19,740

Total Income before Tax = $76,720 + $14,560 + $19,740 = $111,020

Appendix

TABLE A-8

1980 Income Table for the Province of Prince Edward Island

Your Cash Income	Your Full Cash Income	Income from Government	Hidden Income	Hidden Purchasing Power Loss	Total Income Before Tax
		(Dollars per family)			
5000	7740	4719	655	906	9301
5500	8675	5385	605	985	10265
6000	9543	6123	516	1041	11100
6500	10077	6363	488	1153	11718
7000	10182	5968	541	1337	12059
7500	10287	5572	593	1520	12401
8000	10397	5180	648	1704	12749
8500	10842	5011	846	1839	13527
9000	11286	4842	1045	1974	14305
9500	11731	4673	1244	2109	15084
10000	12175	4504	1442	2245	15862
10500	12658	4415	1534	2364	16556
11000	13190	4426	1491	2464	17145
11500	13722	4438	1449	2563	17735
12000	14254	4449	1407	2663	18324
12500	14786	4460	1365	2763	18914
13000	15196	4402	1336	2890	19421
13500	15588	4335	1309	3020	19918
14000	15981	4268	1282	3151	20414
14500	16373	4201	1255	3282	20911
15000	16766	4134	1228	3413	21407
15500	17183	4092	1222	3537	21943
16000	17722	4170	1322	3629	22673
16500	18260	4248	1422	3720	23402
17000	18799	4326	1522	3812	24132
17500	19337	4404	1622	3903	24862
18000	19875	4482	1722	3995	25592
18500	20414	4560	1821	4086	26321
19000	20952	4638	1921	4178	27051
19500	21490	4716	2021	4269	27781
20000	22027	4787	2125	4362	28514
20500	22507	4668	2332	4501	29339
21000	22986	4548	2539	4640	30165
21500	23466	4428	2746	4778	30991
22000	23946	4309	2953	4917	31816
22500	24426	4189	3160	5055	32642
23000	24906	4069	3367	5194	33467
23500	25386	3949	3575	5333	34293
24000	25866	3830	3782	5471	35119
24500	26345	3710	3989	5610	35944
25000	26825	3590	4196	5749	36770

TABLE A-8 continued

1980 Income Table for the Province of Prince Edward Island

Your Cash Income	Your Full Cash Income	Income from Government	Hidden Income	Hidden Purchasing Power Loss	Total Income Before Tax
		(Dollars per family)			
25500	27305	3471	4403	5887	37595
26000	27772	3416	4512	6040	38324
26500	28230	3403	4560	6202	38993
27000	28688	3389	4608	6364	39661
27500	29147	3375	4656	6526	40330
28000	29605	3361	4704	6688	40998
28500	30063	3348	4753	6851	41666
29000	30522	3334	4801	7013	42335
29500	30980	3320	4849	7175	43003
30000	31438	3306	4897	7337	43672
30500	31897	3293	4945	7499	44340
31000	32355	3279	4993	7661	45009
31500	32851	3296	5036	7827	45714
32000	33499	3442	5057	8012	46568
32500	34148	3587	5078	8197	47423
33000	34796	3732	5099	8381	48277
33500	35445	3878	5121	8566	49132
34000	36093	4023	5142	8751	49986
34500	36742	4169	5163	8936	50841
35000	37390	4314	5184	9120	51695
35500	38039	4459	5206	9305	52549
36000	38687	4605	5227	9490	53404
36500	39336	4750	5248	9674	54258
37000	39984	4895	5269	9859	55113
37500	40823	4906	5415	9986	56224
38000	41715	4879	5597	10096	57408
38500	42607	4851	5778	10206	58592
39000	43499	4823	5960	10317	59776
39500	44392	4796	6141	10427	60960
40000	45284	4768	6323	10537	62144
40500	46176	4741	6504	10648	63328
41000	47068	4713	6686	10758	64512
41500	47960	4686	6867	10868	65696
42000	48853	4658	7049	10979	66880
42500	49745	4631	7230	11089	68064
43000	50637	4603	7412	11199	69248
43500	51529	4575	7593	11309	70432
44000	52422	4548	7775	11420	71616
44500	53314	4520	7956	11530	72800
45000	54206	4493	8138	11640	73984

SCHEDULE A-8

1980 Detailed Income Calculation for the Province of Prince Edward Island

Your Cash Income

1. Full Cash Income	= Cash Income x 1.205	=
2. Of which Income from Government	= $4,493	=
3. Hidden Income	= Cash Income x .181	= $ 4,493
4. Hidden Purchasing Power Loss	= Cash Income x .259	=
Total Income before Tax	= 1 + 3 + 4	=
		=

EXAMPLE:

Your Cash Income

1. Full Cash Income	= $70,000 x 1.205	= $ 70,000
2. Of which Income from Government	= $4,493	= $ 84,350
3. Hidden Income	= $70,000 x .181	= $ 4,493
4. Hidden Purchasing Power Loss	= $70,000 x .259	= $ 12,670
		= $ 18,130
Total Income before Tax	= $84,350 + $12,670 + $18,130	= $115,150

TABLE A-9

1980 Income Table for the Province of Quebec

Your Cash Income	Your Full Cash Income	Income from Government	Hidden Income	Hidden Purchasing Power Loss	Total Income Before Tax
		(Dollars per family)			
5000	7054	5165	513	1007	8573
5500	7661	5392	719	1216	9596
6000	8208	5485	1056	1483	10748
6500	8761	5583	134C	1740	11841
7000	9366	5722	1207	1908	12481
7500	9970	5860	1073	2077	13120
8000	10574	5999	940	2246	13760
8500	11107	5934	977	2460	14544
9000	11592	5733	1130	2705	15426
9500	12077	5531	1282	2949	16308
10000	12562	5330	1434	3194	17189
10500	13046	5129	1586	3438	18071
11000	13494	4825	1699	3698	18892
11500	13939	4512	1809	3959	19707
12000	14383	4199	1918	4221	20522
12500	14828	3886	2028	4482	21337
13000	15276	3658	2102	4660	22038
13500	15738	3721	2058	4554	22351
14000	16200	3785	2014	4448	22663
14500	16662	3849	1971	4342	22975
15000	17124	3912	1927	4236	23287
15500	17587	3976	1883	4131	23600
16000	18032	3967	1869	4106	24007
16500	18447	3832	1908	4221	24577
17000	18863	3697	1947	4337	25146
17500	19279	3562	1985	4452	25716
18000	19695	3427	2024	4567	26286
18500	20110	3293	2063	4683	26856
19000	20526	3158	2101	4798	27426
19500	20942	3023	2140	4913	27995
20000	21358	2888	2179	5028	28565
20500	21774	2754	2218	5144	29135
21000	22283	2747	2291	5293	29866
21500	22793	2741	2364	5442	30598
22000	23302	2735	2437	5591	31331
22500	23812	2729	2511	5740	32063
23000	24322	2723	2584	5889	32795
23500	24831	2716	2657	6038	33527
24000	25341	2710	2730	6187	34259
24500	25851	2704	2804	6336	34991
25000	26361	2698	2877	6486	35723

TABLE A-9 continued

Your Cash Income	Your Full Cash Income	Income from Government	Hidden Income	Hidden Purchasing Power Loss	Total Income Before Tax
		(Dollars per family)			
25500	26870	2692	2950	6635	36455
26000	27380	2686	3024	6784	37187
26500	27883	2678	3093	6924	37900
27000	28368	2663	3154	7042	38564
27500	28854	2649	3214	7160	39227
28000	29339	2635	3274	7278	39890
28500	29824	2621	3334	7395	40554
29000	30310	2607	3394	7513	41217
29500	30795	2592	3455	7631	41881
30000	31280	2578	3515	7749	42544
30500	31766	2564	3575	7867	43207
31000	32251	2550	3635	7984	43871
31500	32736	2536	3696	8102	44534
32000	33222	2521	3756	8220	45198
32500	33747	2524	3833	8343	45923
33000	34302	2541	3922	8471	46696
33500	34858	2557	4012	8598	47468
34000	35413	2573	4102	8726	48241
34500	35969	2589	4192	8853	49014
35000	36524	2605	4282	8981	49787
35500	37080	2621	4371	9108	50560
36000	37635	2638	4461	9236	51332
36500	38191	2654	4551	9363	52105
37000	38746	2670	4641	9491	52878
37500	39302	2686	4731	9618	53651
38000	39857	2702	4820	9746	54424
38500	40416	2700	5072	9938	55426
39000	40975	2694	5352	10142	56469
39500	41533	2689	5633	10346	57512
40000	42092	2683	5913	10550	58555
40500	42651	2677	6193	10754	59598
41000	43210	2672	6473	10958	60641
41500	43769	2666	6753	11162	61684
42000	44328	2660	7034	11366	62727
42500	44886	2655	7314	11570	63770
43000	45445	2649	7594	11773	64813
43500	46004	2643	7874	11977	65856
44000	46563	2638	8155	12181	66899
44500	47122	2632	8435	12385	67942
45000	47681	2627	8715	12589	68985

SCHEDULE A-9

1980 Detailed Income Calculation for the Province of Quebec

Your Cash Income

1. Full Cash Income = Cash Income x 1.060 = _____

2. Of which Income from Government = $2,627 = $ 2,627

3. Hidden Income = Cash Income x .194 = _____

4. Hidden Purchasing Power Loss = Cash Income x .280 = _____

Total Income before Tax = 1 + 3 + 4 = _____

EXAMPLE:

Your Cash Income

1. Full Cash Income = $70,000 x 1.060 = $ 70,000

2. Of which Income from Government = $2,627 = $ 74,200

3. Hidden Income = $70,000 x .194 = $ 2,627

4. Hidden Purchasing Power Loss = $70,000 x .280 = $ 13,580

Total Income before Tax = $74,200 + $13,580 + $19,600 = $ 19,600

= $107,380

Appendix

TABLE A-10

1980 Income Table for the Province of Saskatchewan

Your Cash Income	Your Full Cash Income	Income from Government	Hidden Income	Hidden Purchasing Power Loss	Total Income Before Tax
		(Dollars per family)			
5000	7385	3478	1382	2831	11598
5500	8159	3567	1626	3264	13049
6000	8785	3800	1451	3338	13575
6500	9411	4033	1277	3412	14101
7000	10063	4269	1184	3578	14826
7500	10729	4507	1136	3793	15658
8000	11395	4744	1087	4008	16489
8500	12059	4973	1040	4222	17321
9000	12668	4539	1121	4391	18180
9500	13276	4105	1203	4560	19039
10000	13884	3672	1284	4729	19897
10500	14492	3238	1366	4898	20756
11000	15085	2877	1450	5041	21577
11500	15601	2895	1549	5046	22196
12000	16117	2913	1648	5050	22815
12500	16632	2931	1746	5055	23433
13000	17148	2949	1845	5059	24052
13500	17700	2963	1929	5130	24759
14000	18334	2965	1982	5349	25664
14500	18968	2967	2034	5568	26569
15000	19602	2969	2086	5787	27475
15500	20236	2971	2138	6006	28380
16000	20870	2973	2190	6225	29285
16500	21468	2957	2239	6420	30126
17000	21949	2885	2275	6539	30764
17500	22431	2812	2312	6658	31401
18000	22913	2740	2348	6777	32038
18500	23395	2668	2385	6896	32676
19000	23877	2595	2421	7015	33313
19500	24359	2523	2458	7134	33950
20000	24840	2450	2494	7253	34588
20500	25322	2378	2531	7372	35225
21000	25804	2305	2567	7491	35862
21500	26358	2246	2642	7635	36635
22000	26975	2198	2752	7800	37527
22500	27592	2151	2861	7966	38419
23000	28209	2103	2971	8131	39311
23500	28826	2055	3080	8296	40203
24000	29443	2008	3190	8462	41095
24500	30061	1960	3299	8627	41987
25000	30678	1912	3409	8793	42879

TABLE A-10 continued

Your Cash Income	Your Full Cash Income	Income from Government	Hidden Income	Hidden Purchasing Power Loss	Total Income Before Tax
		(Dollars per family)			
25500	31295	1864	3518	8958	43771
26000	31912	1817	3628	9123	44663
26500	32529	1769	3737	9289	45555
27000	33146	1721	3846	9454	46447
27500	33760	1696	3940	9622	47323
28000	34367	1704	4011	9795	48174
28500	34975	1712	4082	9967	49025
29000	35583	1719	4153	10139	49876
29500	36191	1727	4224	10312	50727
30000	36799	1735	4295	10484	51578
30500	37407	1743	4366	10656	52429
31000	38015	1751	4437	10829	53280
31500	38623	1759	4508	11001	54132
32000	39231	1767	4579	11174	54983
32500	39838	1775	4650	11346	55834
33000	40446	1783	4720	11518	56685
33500	41032	1799	4804	11671	57507
34000	41558	1839	4921	11769	58247
34500	42083	1879	5038	11866	58988
35000	42609	1919	5155	11964	59728
35500	43134	1959	5272	12062	60468
36000	43660	1999	5389	12160	61209
36500	44185	2039	5506	12258	61949
37000	44711	2080	5623	12356	62690
37500	45236	2120	5740	12453	63430
38000	45762	2160	5857	12551	64170
38500	46287	2200	5975	12649	64911
39000	46813	2240	6092	12747	65651
39500	47359	2275	6224	12875	66458
40000	48043	2274	6454	13205	67702
40500	48728	2274	6684	13535	68946
41000	49412	2274	6915	13864	70191
41500	50096	2274	7145	14194	71435
42000	50780	2274	7376	14524	72679
42500	51464	2274	7606	14853	73924
43000	52149	2274	7836	15183	75168
43500	52833	2273	8067	15513	76412
44000	53517	2273	8297	15842	77657
44500	54201	2273	8528	16172	78901
45000	54886	2273	8758	16502	80145

SCHEDULE A-10

1980 Detailed Income Calculation for the Province of Saskatchewan

Your Cash Income

1. Full Cash Income	= Cash Income x 1.220	=
2. Of which Income from Government	= $2,273	=
3. Hidden Income	= Cash Income x .195	= $ 2,273
4. Hidden Purchasing Power Loss	= Cash Income x .367	=
Total Income before Tax	= 1 + 3 + 4	=

EXAMPLE:

Your Cash Income

1. Full Cash Income	= $70,000 x 1.220	= $ 70,000
2. Of which Income from Government	= $2,273	= $ 85,400
3. Hidden Income	= $70,000 x .195	= $ 2,273
4. Hidden Purchasing Power Loss	= $70,000 x .367	= $ 13,650
		= $ 25,690
Total Income before Tax	= $85,400 + $13,650 + $25,690	= $124,740

TABLE A-11

1980 Income Table for Canada

Your Cash Income	Your Full Cash Income	Income from Government	Hidden Income	Hidden Purchasing Power Loss	Total Income Before Tax
		(Dollars per family)			
5000	6744	4308	654	1531	8930
5500	7515	4606	773	1756	10044
6000	8131	4712	951	1991	11073
6500	8747	4819	1129	2226	12102
7000	9327	4926	1138	2491	12956
7500	9898	5034	1105	2764	13767
8000	10469	5141	1072	3037	14578
8500	11035	5185	1072	3294	15401
9000	11580	5004	1191	3496	16267
9500	12125	4824	1310	3698	17133
10000	12670	4643	1429	3900	17999
10500	13215	4462	1548	4101	18865
11000	13719	4268	1682	4272	19673
11500	14168	4056	1836	4401	20404
12000	14616	3844	1990	4529	21136
12500	15065	3632	2144	4658	21867
13000	15514	3420	2298	4787	22599
13500	15995	3336	2329	4894	23219
14000	16497	3331	2283	4988	23769
14500	16999	3327	2237	5082	24318
15000	17501	3322	2191	5176	24868
15500	18003	3317	2145	5271	25418
16000	18505	3313	2099	5365	25968
16500	18981	3247	2105	5443	26529
17000	19443	3145	2141	5511	27096
17500	19905	3043	2178	5580	27663
18000	20367	2942	2214	5648	28230
18500	20830	2840	2250	5717	28797
19000	21292	2739	2287	5786	29364
19500	21754	2637	2323	5854	29931
20000	22216	2535	2360	5923	30498
20500	22678	2434	2396	5991	31065
21000	23140	2332	2433	6060	31633
21500	23646	2323	2501	6164	32311
22000	24156	2320	2572	6270	32998
22500	24666	2318	2643	6376	33685
23000	25176	2315	2714	6482	34372
23500	25686	2313	2785	6588	35059
24000	26195	2310	2856	6694	35746

Appendix

TABLE A-11 continued

1980 Income Table for Canada

Your Cash Income	Your Full Cash Income	Income from Government	Hidden Income	Hidden Purchasing Power Loss	Total Income Before Tax
		(Dollars per family)			
24500	26705	2308	2927	6800	36433
25000	27215	2305	2998	6906	37120
25500	27725	2302	3070	7012	37807
26000	28235	2300	3141	7119	38494
26500	28744	2297	3212	7225	39181
27000	29254	2295	3283	7331	39868
27500	29753	2281	3392	7492	40637
28000	30250	2266	3506	7659	41414
28500	30747	2251	3619	7825	42192
29000	31245	2236	3732	7992	42969
29500	31742	2220	3846	8158	43746
30000	32240	2205	3959	8325	44523
30500	32737	2190	4072	8491	45300
31000	33234	2175	4185	8658	46078
31500	33732	2160	4299	8824	46855
32000	34229	2145	4412	8991	47632
32500	34727	2130	4525	9158	48409
33000	35224	2115	4638	9324	49186
33500	35776	2115	4760	9477	50012
34000	36334	2116	4882	9628	50843
34500	36892	2118	5004	9778	51675
35000	37451	2119	5126	9929	52506
35500	38009	2121	5248	10080	53338
36000	38567	2123	5371	10231	54169
36500	39126	2124	5493	10382	55000
37000	39684	2126	5615	10533	55832
37500	40242	2127	5737	10684	56663
38000	40801	2129	5859	10835	57495
38500	41359	2131	5981	10986	58326
39000	41917	2132	6104	11136	59158
39500	42517	2136	6348	11368	60233
40000	43123	2141	6607	11610	61339
40500	43728	2145	6867	11851	62445
41000	44333	2149	7126	12093	63552
41500	44938	2154	7385	12335	64658
42000	45543	2158	7645	12576	65765
42500	46149	2162	7904	12818	66871
43000	46754	2167	8164	13060	67977
43500	47359	2171	8423	13301	69084
44000	47964	2176	8683	13543	70190
44500	48570	2180	8942	13785	71296
45000	49175	2184	9202	14026	72402

SCHEDULE A-11

1980 Detailed Income Calculation for Canada

Your Cash Income

1. Full Cash Income	= Cash Income x 1.093	= _____
2. Of which Income from Government	= $2,184	= $ 2,184
3. Hidden Income	= Cash Income x .205	= _____
4. Hidden Purchasing Power Loss	= Cash Income x .312	= _____
Total Income before Tax	= 1 + 3 + 4	= _____

EXAMPLE:

Your Cash Income

1. Full Cash Income	= $70,000 x 1.093	= $ 70,000
2. Of which Income from Government	= $2,184	= $ 76,510
3. Hidden Income	= $70,000 x .205	= $ 2,184
4. Hidden Purchasing Power Loss	= $70,000 x .312	= $ 14,350
Total Income before Tax	= $76,510 + $14,350 + $21,840	= $ 21,840
		= $112,700

HOW TO USE THE TAX TABLES

Tables A-12 to A-22 are the 1980 Tax Tables for each of the
ten provinces and Canada as a whole. You will be able to
locate within $500 your cash income in the first column of
each Tax Table. You will then be able to establish for the
province in which you reside, how much income you
spent on each tax. The final column shows your total tax
bill.

Step 1. Calculate your family's cash income as you did in Step 1 and Step 2 of
         the income calculation.
Step 2. If your family's cash income exceeded $45,000, skip to Step 5. If not,
         proceed to Step 3.
Step 3. Locate the line in the Tax Table that has your cash income in the first
         column.
         If your cash income was $21,000 for 1980, locate $21,000 in the 1980
         Tax Table for your province of residence.
Step 4. Read off the tax sub-totals and total tax paid.

eg. *Alberta*

Your Cash Income	Profits Tax	Income Tax	Sales Tax	Liquor, Tobacco, Amusement, and Other Excise Taxes	Auto, Fuel, & Motor Vehicle Licence Taxes
$	$	$	$	$	$
21,000	2,758	3,326	461	498	144

Social Security, Medical, & Hospital Taxes	Property Tax	Natural Resources Taxes	Import Duties	Other Taxes	Total Taxes
$	$	$	$	$	$
1,512	885	5,648	456	336	16,024

Step 5. If your cash income exceeded $45,000, you will have to use the
         Detailed Tax Calculation Schedules which accompany each Tax Table.

TABLE A-12

1980 Tax Table for the Province of Alberta

(Dollars per family)

Your Cash Income	Profits Tax	Income Tax	Sales Tax	Liquor, Tobacco, Amusement and Other Excise Taxes	Auto, Fuel & Motor Vehicle Licence Taxes	Social Security, Pension, Medical & Hospital Taxes	Property Tax	Natural Resources Taxes	Import Duties	Other Taxes	Total Taxes
5000	1228	41	50	54	16	512	394	2514	50	84	4943
5500	1444	67	64	69	20	610	463	2957	64	102	5860
6000	1731	126	78	84	24	673	556	3545	77	124	7019
6500	2019	185	92	100	29	736	648	4134	91	146	8179
7000	2225	212	103	111	32	689	714	4555	102	155	8899
7500	2428	239	114	123	35	639	779	4972	113	164	9607
8000	2632	265	125	134	39	589	845	5390	123	174	10314
8500	2681	333	138	149	43	583	860	5489	136	180	10591
9000	2514	459	154	166	48	639	807	5148	152	182	10271
9500	2348	586	170	184	53	695	754	4808	168	185	9951
10000	2182	712	187	201	58	751	700	4468	184	187	9631
10500	2016	839	203	219	63	806	647	4128	201	189	9311
11000	2007	966	217	234	68	855	644	4109	214	198	9512
11500	2071	1094	230	248	72	900	665	4241	227	210	9956
12000	2135	1221	243	262	76	945	685	4372	240	222	10400
12500	2199	1349	256	276	80	990	706	4503	252	234	10843
13000	2263	1477	268	289	84	1034	726	4634	265	246	11287
13500	2300	1589	281	303	87	1064	738	4710	277	251	11601
14000	2336	1701	293	316	91	1092	750	4783	290	256	11908
14500	2372	1812	306	330	95	1120	761	4856	302	261	12215
15000	2407	1924	318	343	99	1149	772	4929	314	266	12521
15500	2443	2035	331	357	103	1177	784	5002	327	271	12828
16000	2478	2147	343	370	107	1205	795	5074	339	276	13134

TABLE A-12 continued

(Dollars per family)

Your Cash Income	Profits Tax	Income Tax	Sales Tax	Liquor, Tobacco, Amusement and Other Excise Taxes	Auto, Fuel & Motor Vehicle Licence Taxes	Social Security, Pension, Medical & Hospital Taxes	Property Tax	Natural Resources Taxes	Import Duties	Other Taxes	Total Taxes
16500	2508	2264	355	383	110	1235	805	5135	351	282	13428
17000	2537	2382	367	396	114	1266	814	5196	362	288	13722
17500	2567	2499	379	408	118	1296	824	5256	374	294	14015
18000	2597	2616	391	421	122	1326	833	5317	386	300	14309
18500	2626	2734	403	434	125	1356	843	5378	398	306	14603
19000	2656	2851	414	447	129	1387	852	5438	409	312	14896
19500	2686	2969	426	460	133	1417	862	5499	421	318	15190
20000	2715	3086	438	473	136	1447	871	5560	433	324	15484
20500	2745	3203	450	485	140	1477	881	5621	445	330	15778
21000	2758	3327	462	498	144	1512	885	5648	456	336	16024
21500	2758	3455	473	510	147	1550	885	5647	467	341	16232
22000	2758	3582	484	522	151	1588	885	5646	478	346	16440
22500	2757	3710	495	534	154	1627	885	5646	489	351	16649
23000	2757	3838	506	546	158	1665	885	5645	500	356	16857
23500	2757	3966	518	558	161	1703	885	5645	511	362	17065
24000	2756	4094	529	570	165	1742	884	5644	522	367	17273
24500	2756	4222	540	582	168	1780	884	5643	533	372	17481
25000	2756	4350	551	594	172	1818	884	5643	544	377	17689
25500	2755	4478	562	606	175	1856	884	5642	555	382	17897
26000	2755	4606	574	618	178	1895	884	5641	566	387	18105
26500	2755	4733	585	631	182	1933	884	5641	577	393	18313
27000	2830	4868	596	643	185	1969	908	5795	589	402	18786
27500	2937	5005	607	655	189	2005	942	6014	600	412	19368
28000	3044	5143	619	667	193	2041	977	6233	611	422	19950
28500	3151	5280	630	680	196	2077	1011	6452	622	433	20532
29000	3258	5417	642	692	200	2113	1045	6671	634	443	21115

21697	454	645	6890	1080	2148	203	704	653	5555	3365	29500
22279	464	656	7109	1114	2184	207	716	664	5692	3472	30000
22861	475	667	7328	1148	2220	210	729	676	5829	3579	30500
23444	485	679	7547	1183	2256	214	741	687	5967	3686	31000
24026	496	690	7766	1217	2292	217	753	698	6104	3793	31500
24608	506	701	7985	1251	2327	221	766	710	6241	3900	32000
25190	517	712	8204	1286	2363	224	778	721	6379	4007	32500
25640	527	724	8332	1306	2406	228	790	733	6526	4069	33000
26068	537	735	8445	1323	2450	232	802	744	6675	4124	33500
26497	547	746	8559	1341	2494	235	815	756	6825	4180	34000
26925	557	758	8672	1359	2538	239	827	767	6974	4235	34500
27354	568	769	8785	1377	2581	242	839	778	7123	4291	35000
27782	578	780	8899	1395	2625	246	852	790	7272	4346	35500
28211	588	791	9012	1412	2669	249	864	801	7422	4401	36000
28639	598	803	9126	1430	2713	253	876	813	7571	4457	36500
29068	608	814	9239	1448	2757	256	889	824	7720	4512	37000
29496	619	825	9352	1466	2801	260	901	836	7869	4567	37500
29925	629	837	9466	1483	2845	264	913	847	8019	4623	38000
30358	639	848	9582	1502	2888	267	926	858	8168	4680	38500
31008	649	858	9854	1544	2915	270	936	868	8300	4812	39000
31657	659	868	10125	1587	2942	273	947	878	8433	4945	39500
32307	669	877	10396	1629	2969	276	958	888	8566	5077	40000
32957	679	887	10668	1672	2996	280	969	898	8699	5210	40500
33607	690	897	10939	1714	3023	283	979	908	8831	5342	41000
34257	700	907	11210	1757	3050	286	990	918	8964	5475	41500
34907	710	917	11482	1799	3077	289	1001	928	9097	5607	42000
35557	720	927	11753	1842	3104	292	1012	938	9230	5740	42500
36206	730	936	12024	1884	3131	295	1022	948	9362	5872	43000
36856	740	946	12296	1927	3157	298	1033	958	9495	6005	43500
37506	750	956	12567	1969	3184	301	1044	968	9628	6137	44000
38156	760	966	12838	2012	3211	304	1055	978	9761	6270	44500
38806	770	976	13110	2054	3238	307	1066	988	9893	6402	45000

SCHEDULE A-12

1980 Detailed Tax Calculation for the Province of Alberta

1. Profit tax	= Your Cash Income x .142	=
2. Income tax	= Your Cash Income x .220	=
3. Sales tax	= Your Cash Income x .022	=
4. Liquor, tobacco, amusement & other excise taxes	= Your Cash Income x .024	=
5. Auto, fuel & motor vehicle licence fees	= Your Cash Income x .007	=
6. Social security, pension, medical & hospital taxes	= Your Cash Income x .072	=
7. Property tax	= Your Cash Income x .046	=
8. Natural resources taxes	= Your Cash Income x .291	=
9. Import duties	= Your Cash Income x .022	=
10. Other taxes	= Your Cash Income x .017	=

Total taxes   1 + 2 + 3 + 4 + 5 + 6 + 7 + 8 + 9 + 10   =

TABLE A-13

1980 Tax Table for the Province of British Columbia

(Dollars per family)

Your Cash Income	Profits Tax	Income Tax	Sales Tax	Liquor, Tobacco, Amusement and Other Excise Taxes	Auto, Fuel & Motor Vehicle Licence Taxes	Social Security, Pension, Medical & Hospital Taxes	Property Tax	Natural Resources Taxes	Import Duties	Other Taxes	Total Taxes
5000	298	34	124	37	28	440	319	160	35	34	1510
5500	323	40	143	43	32	535	345	174	40	39	1715
6000	364	88	200	60	45	653	389	196	56	54	2105
6500	405	138	257	77	58	772	433	218	72	70	2501
7000	499	173	288	86	65	779	534	269	81	79	2855
7500	643	195	294	88	66	681	688	346	83	83	3168
8000	787	217	300	90	68	583	841	424	84	86	3481
8500	931	239	306	92	69	485	995	501	86	90	3794
9000	951	331	333	100	75	499	1016	512	94	94	4005
9500	945	437	365	109	83	535	1010	509	103	99	4196
10000	940	543	397	119	90	570	1005	506	112	104	4387
10500	935	649	429	129	97	606	999	503	121	109	4578
11000	930	755	461	138	104	642	994	500	130	114	4769
11500	931	862	502	150	113	683	995	501	141	122	5003
12000	934	969	543	163	123	725	998	502	153	131	5240
12500	936	1076	585	175	132	766	1000	504	164	139	5478
13000	938	1183	626	188	141	808	1002	505	176	148	5715
13500	942	1290	667	200	151	849	1007	507	188	156	5956
14000	1016	1383	704	211	159	873	1085	547	198	164	6339
14500	1089	1477	740	222	167	897	1164	586	208	172	6721
15000	1163	1570	776	233	175	920	1243	626	218	179	7103
15500	1236	1664	813	243	184	944	1321	665	229	187	7485
16000	1310	1757	849	254	192	968	1400	705	239	194	7868

TABLE A-13 continued

Your Cash Income	Profits Tax	Income Tax	Sales Tax	Liquor, Tobacco, Amusement and Other Excise Taxes	Auto, Fuel & Motor Vehicle Licence Taxes	Social Security, Pension, Medical & Hospital Taxes	Property Tax	Natural Resources Taxes	Import Duties	Other Taxes	Total Taxes
				(Dollars per family)							
16500	1383	1850	885	265	200	992	1478	745	249	202	8250
17000	1350	1948	921	276	208	1015	1443	727	259	206	8357
17500	1304	2047	957	287	216	1046	1394	702	269	210	8433
18000	1259	2145	993	298	224	1074	1345	677	279	214	8509
18500	1213	2244	1029	308	233	1101	1296	653	289	218	8585
19000	1168	2342	1065	319	241	1128	1248	628	300	222	8661
19500	1122	2440	1101	330	249	1156	1199	604	310	226	8737
20000	1077	2539	1137	341	257	1183	1150	579	320	230	8813
20500	1031	2637	1173	351	265	1211	1102	555	330	234	8889
21000	985	2736	1209	362	273	1238	1053	530	340	238	8965
21500	943	2835	1244	373	281	1266	1008	508	350	242	9051
22000	937	2942	1272	381	287	1296	1001	504	358	247	9225
22500	930	3049	1300	389	294	1326	994	501	366	252	9400
23000	923	3156	1327	398	300	1356	987	497	373	256	9574
23500	917	3263	1355	406	306	1386	980	493	381	261	9749
24000	910	3371	1383	414	312	1416	973	490	389	266	9923
24500	903	3478	1410	423	319	1446	966	486	397	270	10098
25000	897	3585	1438	431	325	1476	958	483	404	275	10273
25500	890	3692	1466	439	331	1506	951	479	412	280	10447
26000	884	3799	1493	447	337	1536	944	476	420	285	10622
26500	877	3906	1521	456	344	1566	937	472	428	289	10796
27000	870	4014	1549	464	350	1597	930	468	436	294	10971
27500	864	4121	1576	472	356	1627	923	465	443	299	11145
28000	894	4235	1608	482	363	1660	955	481	452	305	11435
28500	931	4350	1640	491	371	1694	995	501	461	312	11747
29000	969	4465	1672	501	378	1728	1036	522	470	319	12060

Income											
29500	12372	325	479	542	1076	1763	385	511	1705	4580	1007
30000	12685	332	488	562	1116	1797	392	520	1737	4695	1044
30500	12997	339	498	582	1156	1831	400	530	1769	4810	1082
31000	13310	346	507	603	1197	1865	407	540	1801	4925	1120
31500	13622	352	516	623	1237	1899	414	549	1834	5040	1157
32000	13935	359	525	643	1277	1934	422	559	1866	5155	1195
32500	14247	366	534	664	1317	1968	429	569	1898	5270	1233
33000	14560	373	543	684	1358	2002	436	578	1930	5385	1270
33500	14872	380	552	704	1398	2036	443	588	1963	5500	1308
34000	15108	386	561	707	1404	2073	451	597	1994	5621	1314
34500	15288	391	570	698	1386	2111	458	607	2025	5746	1297
35000	15467	397	578	688	1367	2149	465	616	2056	5871	1279
35500	15646	402	587	679	1348	2188	472	625	2087	5996	1261
36000	15825	408	596	669	1329	2226	479	635	2118	6122	1244
36500	16004	414	604	660	1310	2264	486	644	2149	6247	1226
37000	16184	419	613	651	1292	2303	493	653	2180	6372	1209
37500	16363	425	622	641	1273	2341	500	662	2211	6497	1191
38000	16542	431	631	632	1254	2379	507	672	2242	6622	1174
38500	16721	436	639	622	1235	2417	514	681	2274	6747	1156
39000	16900	442	648	613	1217	2456	521	690	2304	6872	1138
39500	17079	447	657	603	1198	2494	528	700	2335	6997	1121
40000	17311	454	665	607	1205	2526	534	709	2366	7118	1127
40500	17656	462	674	639	1268	2544	541	718	2395	7229	1187
41000	18001	470	682	671	1332	2561	548	726	2425	7340	1246
41500	18346	479	690	703	1395	2579	554	735	2454	7452	1305
42000	18691	487	698	734	1458	2597	561	744	2483	7563	1365
42500	19036	495	707	766	1522	2615	568	753	2513	7674	1424
43000	19381	503	715	798	1585	2633	574	762	2542	7785	1483
43500	19726	512	723	830	1648	2650	581	770	2572	7897	1543
44000	20071	520	732	862	1712	2668	588	779	2601	8008	1602
44500	20417	528	740	894	1775	2686	594	788	2631	8119	1661
45000	20762	536	748	926	1839	2704	601	797	2660	8230	1721

SCHEDULE A-13

1980 Detailed Tax Calculation for the Province of British Columbia

1. Profit tax	= Your Cash Income x .038	
2. Income tax	= Your Cash Income x .183	
3. Sales tax	= Your Cash Income x .059	
4. Liquor, tobacco, amusement & other excise taxes	= Your Cash Income x .018	
5. Auto, fuel & motor vehicle licence fees	= Your Cash Income x .013	
6. Social security, pension, medical & hospital taxes	= Your Cash Income x .060	
7. Property tax	= Your Cash Income x .041	
8. Natural resources taxes	= Your Cash Income x .021	
9. Import duties	= Your Cash Income x .017	
10. Other taxes	= Your Cash Income x .012	

Total taxes   1 + 2 + 3 + 4 + 5 + 6 + 7 + 8 + 9 + 10   =

TABLE A-14

1980 Tax Table for the Province of Manitoba

(Dollars per family)

Your Cash Income	Profits Tax	Income Tax	Sales Tax	Liquor, Tobacco, Amusement and Other Excise Taxes	Auto, Fuel & Motor Vehicle Licence Taxes	Social Security, Pension, Medical & Hospital Taxes	Property Tax	Natural Resources Taxes	Import Duties	Other Taxes	Total Taxes
5000	531	37	150	68	56	140	708	47	58	101	1897
5500	624	48	176	80	65	165	832	56	68	119	2231
6000	677	102	176	80	66	159	902	60	68	125	2416
6500	730	157	177	80	66	154	973	65	68	132	2602
7000	727	191	200	91	74	186	969	65	77	140	2721
7500	693	215	237	108	88	238	924	62	91	149	2805
8000	658	239	274	124	102	289	878	59	106	158	2888
8500	624	264	310	141	115	341	833	56	120	167	2972
9000	699	380	345	157	128	378	932	62	133	185	3399
9500	773	496	379	172	141	415	1032	69	146	203	3826
10000	848	612	413	188	153	452	1131	76	159	221	4253
10500	923	728	447	203	166	489	1230	82	172	239	4680
11000	990	844	480	218	179	526	1321	89	185	256	5088
11500	1017	962	509	231	189	561	1357	91	196	267	5381
12000	1045	1079	538	244	200	596	1393	93	207	278	5674
12500	1072	1196	567	258	211	631	1430	96	219	288	5967
13000	1099	1313	596	271	222	666	1466	98	230	299	6260
13500	1108	1426	625	284	232	703	1478	99	241	309	6504
14000	1071	1529	654	297	243	745	1428	96	252	315	6630
14500	1033	1631	683	310	254	788	1378	92	263	322	6755
15000	996	1733	713	324	265	830	1328	89	275	328	6881
15500	959	1836	742	337	276	873	1278	86	286	334	7006
16000	921	1938	771	350	287	915	1229	82	297	341	7131

TABLE A-14 continued

Your Cash Income	Profits Tax	Income Tax	Sales Tax	Liquor, Tobacco, Amusement and Other Excise Taxes	Auto, Fuel & Motor Vehicle Licence Taxes	Social Security, Pension, Medical & Hospital Taxes	Property Tax	Natural Resources Taxes	Import Duties	Other Taxes	Total Taxes
						(Dollars per family)					
16500	886	2042	800	363	297	957	1182	79	308	347	7261
17000	859	2149	826	375	307	994	1146	77	318	353	7405
17500	832	2257	852	387	317	1032	1110	74	329	358	7548
18000	805	2365	879	399	327	1069	1074	72	339	364	7692
18500	778	2473	905	411	336	1107	1038	70	349	369	7836
19000	751	2581	931	423	346	1144	1002	67	359	375	7980
19500	724	2688	958	435	356	1182	966	65	369	380	8123
20000	697	2796	984	447	366	1219	930	62	379	386	8267
20500	670	2904	1011	459	376	1257	894	60	390	391	8411
21000	643	3012	1037	471	385	1295	857	57	400	397	8554
21500	647	3125	1063	483	395	1329	864	58	410	405	8779
22000	683	3242	1089	495	405	1359	911	61	420	417	9082
22500	719	3359	1115	507	415	1389	959	64	430	429	9386
23000	755	3477	1141	518	424	1420	1007	67	440	441	9690
23500	790	3594	1167	530	434	1450	1054	71	450	452	9993
24000	826	3712	1193	542	444	1480	1102	74	460	464	10297
24500	862	3829	1219	554	453	1511	1150	77	470	476	10601
25000	898	3947	1245	566	463	1541	1197	80	480	488	10905
25500	933	4064	1271	578	473	1572	1245	83	490	500	11208
26000	969	4181	1297	589	482	1602	1293	87	500	511	11512
26500	1005	4299	1323	601	492	1632	1340	90	510	523	11816
27000	1041	4416	1349	613	502	1663	1388	93	520	535	12119
27500	1062	4537	1375	625	511	1694	1417	95	530	545	12391
28000	1059	4663	1399	636	520	1726	1413	95	540	554	12605
28500	1057	4789	1424	647	529	1759	1409	94	549	563	12819
29000	1054	4915	1448	658	538	1791	1405	94	558	571	13033

Income											
29500	1051	5041	1473	669	547	1824	1401	94	568	580	13248
30000	1048	5167	1497	680	557	1856	1397	94	577	589	13462
30500	1045	5293	1521	691	566	1889	1393	93	586	597	13676
31000	1042	5419	1546	702	575	1921	1390	93	596	606	13890
31500	1039	5546	1570	714	584	1954	1386	93	605	615	14104
32000	1036	5672	1595	725	593	1986	1382	93	615	623	14319
32500	1033	5798	1619	736	602	2019	1378	92	624	632	14533
33000	1030	5924	1644	747	611	2051	1374	92	634	641	14747
33500	1038	6052	1669	758	620	2083	1384	93	643	651	14992
34000	1085	6189	1695	770	630	2113	1447	97	653	667	15346
34500	1131	6326	1721	782	640	2142	1509	101	663	683	15700
35000	1178	6463	1747	794	650	2172	1571	105	674	699	16053
35500	1225	6600	1774	806	659	2201	1634	109	684	715	16407
36000	1272	6738	1800	818	669	2231	1696	114	694	731	16761
36500	1318	6875	1826	830	679	2260	1758	118	704	747	17115
37000	1365	7012	1853	842	689	2290	1821	122	714	763	17469
37500	1412	7149	1879	854	698	2319	1883	126	724	779	17823
38000	1458	7286	1905	866	708	2349	1945	130	734	795	18177
38500	1505	7423	1931	878	718	2378	2007	135	744	811	18530
39000	1552	7560	1958	889	728	2408	2070	139	755	827	18884
39500	1597	7696	1984	901	737	2437	2130	143	765	843	19234
40000	1628	7818	2007	912	746	2465	2171	146	774	865	19531
40500	1659	7940	2030	923	755	2492	2212	148	783	887	19829
41000	1689	8061	2054	933	764	2520	2253	151	792	909	20126
41500	1720	8183	2077	944	772	2547	2294	154	801	931	20423
42000	1750	8305	2101	955	781	2575	2334	156	810	953	20721
42500	1781	8427	2124	965	790	2602	2375	159	819	975	21018
43000	1812	8549	2148	976	798	2630	2416	162	828	997	21315
43500	1842	8671	2171	986	807	2657	2457	165	837	1019	21613
44000	1873	8793	2194	997	816	2685	2498	167	846	1041	21910
44500	1903	8915	2218	1008	824	2713	2539	170	855	1063	22208
45000	1934	9037	2241	1018	833	2740	2579	173	864	1086	22505

SCHEDULE A-14

1980 Detailed Tax Calculation for the Province of Manitoba

1. Profit tax	= Your Cash Income x .043	____
2. Income tax	= Your Cash Income x .201	____
3. Sales tax	= Your Cash Income x .050	____
4. Liquor, tobacco, amusement & other excise taxes	= Your Cash Income x .023	____
5. Auto, fuel & motor vehicle licence fees	= Your Cash Income x .019	____
6. Social security, pension, medical & hospital taxes	= Your Cash Income x .061	____
7. Property tax	= Your Cash Income x .057	____
8. Natural resources taxes	= Your Cash Income x .004	____
9. Import duties	= Your Cash Income x .019	____
10. Other taxes	= Your Cash Income x .024	____

Total taxes   1 + 2 + 3 + 4 + 5 + 6 + 7 + 8 + 9 + 10   = ____

TABLE A-15

1980 Tax Table for the Province of New Brunswick

(Dollars per family)

Your Cash Income	Profits Tax	Income Tax	Sales Tax	Liquor, Tobacco, Amusement and Other Excise Taxes	Auto, Fuel & Motor Vehicle Licence Taxes	Social Security, Pension, Medical & Hospital Taxes	Property Tax	Natural Resources Taxes	Import Duties	Other Taxes	Total Taxes
5000	322	39	177	71	58	140	394	31	55	22	1309
5500	336	82	187	75	61	147	411	32	58	24	1413
6000	343	136	190	76	62	150	419	33	59	25	1496
6500	357	175	215	86	70	174	436	34	67	28	1643
7000	377	199	262	105	86	220	461	36	82	32	1860
7500	398	223	309	124	101	266	486	38	96	36	2077
8000	419	254	356	142	116	312	512	40	111	40	2302
8500	440	369	407	163	133	362	538	42	127	46	2627
9000	462	484	457	183	150	412	565	44	143	52	2952
9500	484	600	508	203	166	462	591	46	158	58	3276
10000	505	715	559	223	183	512	617	48	174	65	3601
10500	499	831	606	242	198	562	610	47	189	69	3853
11000	468	947	649	260	212	612	571	44	202	72	4037
11500	436	1063	692	277	226	661	533	41	216	75	4222
12000	405	1180	736	294	241	711	495	38	229	78	4407
12500	373	1296	779	312	255	761	456	35	243	81	4592
13000	398	1398	826	331	270	807	486	38	258	84	4895
13500	423	1500	874	349	286	852	517	40	272	87	5201
14000	449	1601	921	368	301	898	548	43	287	90	5507
14500	474	1703	968	387	317	944	580	45	302	93	5813
15000	500	1805	1016	406	332	990	611	47	316	96	6119
15500	517	1908	1061	424	347	1035	632	49	331	99	6404
16000	515	2015	1103	441	361	1079	629	49	344	103	6637

TABLE A-15 continued

(Dollars per family)

Your Cash Income	Profits Tax	Income Tax	Sales Tax	Liquor, Tobacco, Amusement and Other Excise Taxes	Auto, Fuel & Motor Vehicle Licence Taxes	Social Security, Pension, Medical & Hospital Taxes	Property Tax	Natural Resources Taxes	Import Duties	Other Taxes	Total Taxes
16500	512	2122	1144	458	374	1123	626	49	357	106	6870
17000	510	2229	1186	474	388	1166	623	48	370	110	7104
17500	507	2336	1228	491	401	1210	620	48	383	113	7337
18000	504	2443	1269	508	415	1254	616	48	396	117	7570
18500	502	2550	1311	524	429	1298	613	48	409	120	7803
19000	499	2657	1353	541	442	1342	610	47	422	124	8037
19500	497	2764	1394	558	456	1386	607	47	434	127	8270
20000	496	2873	1436	574	470	1429	606	47	447	131	8509
20500	502	2989	1479	591	483	1473	613	48	461	135	8773
21000	507	3106	1521	608	497	1516	620	48	474	139	9037
21500	513	3223	1563	625	511	1560	627	49	487	143	9301
22000	519	3339	1606	642	525	1603	634	49	500	147	9566
22500	525	3456	1648	659	539	1647	641	50	514	151	9830
23000	531	3572	1691	676	553	1690	648	50	527	155	10094
23500	537	3689	1733	693	567	1734	656	51	540	159	10358
24000	542	3805	1776	710	581	1777	663	51	553	164	10622
24500	548	3922	1818	727	594	1821	670	52	566	168	10887
25000	554	4039	1860	744	608	1864	677	53	580	172	11151
25500	560	4155	1903	761	622	1908	684	53	593	176	11415
26000	565	4279	1942	777	635	1948	691	54	605	180	11675
26500	570	4404	1980	792	648	1987	697	54	617	184	11934
27000	576	4529	2019	808	660	2027	703	55	629	188	12193
27500	581	4654	2057	823	673	2066	710	55	641	192	12452
28000	586	4779	2096	838	685	2105	716	56	653	196	12711
28500	591	4905	2134	854	698	2145	722	56	665	200	12970
29000	596	5030	2173	869	710	2184	729	57	677	204	13229

Income											
29500	602	5155	2211	884	723	2224	735	57	689	208	13488
30000	607	5280	2250	900	736	2263	741	58	701	212	13747
30500	612	5405	2288	915	748	2302	748	58	713	216	14006
31000	617	5530	2326	931	761	2342	754	59	725	221	14265
31500	649	5660	2368	947	774	2381	793	62	738	227	14599
32000	715	5796	2414	966	789	2419	873	68	752	235	15028
32500	780	5932	2460	984	804	2458	954	74	766	244	15456
33000	846	6068	2505	1002	819	2496	1034	80	781	252	15885
33500	912	6205	2551	1020	834	2535	1114	87	795	261	16314
34000	978	6341	2597	1039	849	2573	1195	93	809	269	16743
34500	1044	6477	2643	1057	864	2612	1275	99	823	278	17171
35000	1109	6613	2688	1075	879	2650	1355	105	838	286	17600
35500	1175	6749	2734	1094	894	2689	1436	111	852	295	18029
36000	1241	6885	2780	1112	909	2727	1516	118	866	303	18458
36500	1307	7021	2826	1130	924	2766	1597	124	881	312	18886
37000	1369	7156	2871	1148	939	2804	1673	130	895	320	19304
37500	1381	7277	2907	1163	950	2840	1687	131	906	329	19569
38000	1392	7398	2942	1177	962	2875	1701	132	917	337	19833
38500	1404	7519	2978	1191	974	2911	1715	133	928	346	20098
39000	1415	7640	3014	1205	985	2946	1729	134	939	354	20362
39500	1427	7761	3049	1220	997	2982	1743	135	950	363	20627
40000	1438	7882	3085	1234	1009	3018	1757	136	961	371	20891
40500	1450	8003	3121	1248	1020	3053	1771	137	972	380	21156
41000	1461	8124	3156	1262	1032	3089	1785	139	984	388	21420
41500	1473	8245	3192	1277	1044	3125	1799	140	995	397	21685
42000	1484	8366	3228	1291	1055	3160	1813	141	1006	405	21949
42500	1496	8487	3263	1305	1067	3196	1827	142	1017	413	22213
43000	1507	8608	3299	1320	1079	3231	1841	143	1028	422	22478
43500	1519	8729	3335	1334	1090	3267	1855	144	1039	430	22742
44000	1530	8850	3370	1348	1102	3303	1869	145	1050	439	23007
44500	1542	8971	3406	1362	1114	3338	1883	146	1061	447	23271
45000	1553	9092	3442	1377	1125	3374	1897	147	1072	456	23536

SCHEDULE A-15

1980 Detailed Tax Calculation for the Province of New Brunswick

1. Profit tax	= Your Cash Income x .035	_____
2. Income tax	= Your Cash Income x .202	_____
3. Sales tax	= Your Cash Income x .077	_____
4. Liquor, tobacco, amusement & other excise taxes	= Your Cash Income x .031	_____
5. Auto, fuel & motor vehicle licence fees	= Your Cash Income x .025	_____
6. Social security, pension, medical & hospital taxes	= Your Cash Income x .075	_____
7. Property tax	= Your Cash Income x .042	_____
8. Natural resources taxes	= Your Cash Income x .003	_____
9. Import duties	= Your Cash Income x .024	_____
10. Other taxes	= Your Cash Income x .010	_____
Total taxes 1 + 2 + 3 + 4 + 5 + 6 + 7 + 8 + 9 + 10		= _____

TABLE A-16

1980 Tax Table for the Province of Newfoundland

Your Cash Income	Profits Tax	Income Tax	Sales Tax	Liquor, Tobacco, Amusement and Other Excise Taxes	Auto, Fuel & Motor Vehicle Licence Taxes	Social Security, Pension, Medical & Hospital Taxes	Property Tax	Natural Resources Taxes	Import Duties	Other Taxes	Total Taxes
					(Dollars per family)						
5000	129	36	117	28	37	93	54	29	34	38	594
5500	152	53	131	32	41	103	64	34	38	45	692
6000	246	106	143	35	45	107	103	55	41	63	943
6500	340	159	155	38	49	110	143	75	44	81	1193
7000	433	187	212	52	67	153	182	96	61	97	1541
7500	527	210	279	68	88	204	222	117	80	114	1909
8000	620	233	346	84	109	256	261	138	99	130	2277
8500	696	277	412	100	129	307	293	154	118	146	2632
9000	710	389	470	114	147	357	299	157	135	162	2941
9500	723	502	529	129	166	408	305	161	152	178	3251
10000	737	614	587	143	184	458	311	164	169	194	3560
10500	751	726	646	157	202	508	317	167	185	210	3869
11000	748	839	700	170	219	555	315	166	201	216	4130
11500	721	953	749	182	235	600	304	160	215	211	4328
12000	695	1066	797	194	250	644	293	154	229	205	4527
12500	668	1179	846	206	265	689	282	148	243	199	4726
13000	642	1293	895	218	280	734	270	142	257	194	4924
13500	618	1397	944	230	296	778	260	137	271	195	5126
14000	595	1496	994	242	312	824	251	132	285	199	5329
14500	573	1595	1044	254	327	869	241	127	300	204	5533
15000	550	1694	1093	266	343	914	232	122	314	208	5736
15500	527	1793	1143	278	358	959	222	117	328	213	5940
16000	505	1892	1193	290	374	1004	213	112	342	218	6143

TABLE A-16 continued

(Dollars per family)

Your Cash Income	Profits Tax	Income Tax	Sales Tax	Liquor, Tobacco, Amusement and Other Excise Taxes	Auto, Fuel & Motor Vehicle Licence Taxes	Social Security, Pension, Medical & Hospital Taxes	Property Tax	Natural Resources Taxes	Import Duties	Other Taxes	Total Taxes
16500	483	1994	1239	301	388	1046	203	107	356	220	6338
17000	461	2099	1282	312	402	1086	194	102	368	222	6528
17500	439	2203	1326	322	416	1126	185	97	381	224	6719
18000	417	2307	1370	333	429	1166	176	93	393	225	6910
18500	395	2412	1414	344	443	1205	167	88	406	227	7100
19000	374	2516	1457	354	457	1245	157	83	418	229	7291
19500	352	2620	1501	365	470	1285	148	78	431	231	7481
20000	330	2725	1545	376	484	1325	139	73	443	232	7672
20500	308	2829	1588	386	498	1365	130	68	456	234	7862
21000	289	2934	1633	397	512	1405	122	64	469	236	8060
21500	310	3048	1683	409	527	1447	130	69	483	246	8351
22000	330	3161	1733	421	543	1489	139	73	497	255	8642
22500	350	3275	1783	434	559	1532	148	78	512	264	8933
23000	371	3388	1833	446	575	1574	156	82	526	274	9224
23500	391	3502	1883	458	590	1616	165	87	541	283	9515
24000	411	3615	1933	470	606	1658	173	91	555	292	9806
24500	432	3729	1983	482	622	1701	182	96	569	302	10097
25000	452	3842	2033	494	637	1743	190	100	584	311	10388
25500	472	3956	2084	507	653	1785	199	105	598	320	10679
26000	493	4070	2134	519	669	1827	208	109	613	330	10970
26500	513	4183	2184	531	684	1870	216	114	627	339	11261
27000	531	4298	2234	543	700	1912	224	118	641	349	11550
27500	529	4420	2283	555	716	1955	223	117	656	363	11816
28000	526	4541	2333	567	731	1999	222	117	670	377	12083
28500	523	4663	2383	579	747	2042	220	116	684	391	12349
29000	521	4785	2432	591	762	2086	219	116	698	405	12616

29500	518	4907	2482	603	778	2130	218	115	712	419	12882
30000	515	5029	2531	615	793	2173	217	114	727	433	13149
30500	513	5151	2581	628	809	2217	216	114	741	447	13415
31000	510	5273	2630	640	824	2260	215	113	755	461	13682
31500	507	5395	2680	652	840	2304	214	113	769	475	13948
32000	505	5517	2729	664	856	2347	213	112	784	489	14215
32500	502	5639	2779	676	871	2391	212	111	798	503	14481
33000	510	5762	2828	688	886	2433	215	113	812	517	14764
33500	597	5895	2873	699	900	2465	252	133	825	538	15176
34000	685	6027	2917	709	914	2498	289	152	838	559	15588
34500	773	6160	2962	720	928	2530	325	171	850	579	16000
35000	860	6293	3007	731	942	2563	362	191	863	600	16412
35500	948	6425	3051	742	956	2595	399	210	876	621	16825
36000	1036	6558	3096	753	970	2627	436	230	889	641	17237
36500	1124	6690	3141	764	984	2660	473	249	902	662	17649
37000	1211	6823	3185	775	998	2692	510	269	914	683	18061
37500	1299	6956	3230	785	1012	2725	547	288	927	703	18473
38000	1387	7088	3275	796	1026	2757	584	308	940	724	18885
38500	1474	7221	3319	807	1040	2790	621	327	953	745	19297
39000	1556	7351	3363	818	1054	2822	656	345	965	766	19697
39500	1599	7469	3401	827	1066	2851	674	355	976	795	20014
40000	1643	7587	3439	836	1078	2881	692	365	987	823	20331
40500	1686	7705	3477	845	1090	2911	710	374	998	852	20649
41000	1729	7823	3515	855	1102	2941	728	384	1009	880	20966
41500	1773	7941	3553	864	1114	2971	747	393	1020	909	21284
42000	1816	8059	3591	873	1125	3001	765	403	1031	937	21601
42500	1859	8177	3629	882	1137	3031	783	413	1042	966	21918
43000	1903	8295	3667	892	1149	3061	801	422	1053	994	22236
43500	1946	8412	3704	901	1161	3091	820	432	1064	1023	22553
44000	1989	8530	3742	910	1173	3120	838	441	1074	1051	22870
44500	2032	8648	3780	919	1185	3150	856	451	1085	1080	23188
45000	2076	8766	3818	928	1197	3180	874	461	1096	1108	23505

Appendix

SCHEDULE A-16

**1980 Detailed Tax Calculation for the
Province of Newfoundland**

1. Profit tax	= Your Cash Income x .046	
2. Income tax	= Your Cash Income x .195	
3. Sales tax	= Your Cash Income x .085	
4. Liquor, tobacco, amusement & other excise taxes	= Your Cash Income x .021	
5. Auto, fuel & motor vehicle licence fees	= Your Cash Income x .027	
6. Social security, pension, medical & hospital taxes	= Your Cash Income x .071	
7. Property tax	= Your Cash Income x .019	
8. Natural resources taxes	= Your Cash Income x .010	
9. Import duties	= Your Cash Income x .024	
10. Other taxes	= Your Cash Income x .025	

Total taxes $1 + 2 + 3 + 4 + 5 + 6 + 7 + 8 + 9 + 10$ =

TABLE A-17

1980 Tax Table for the Province of Nova Scotia

(Dollars per family)

Your Cash Income	Profits Tax	Income Tax	Sales Tax	Liquor, Tobacco, Amusement and Other Excise Taxes	Auto, Fuel & Motor Vehicle Licence Taxes	Social Security, Pension, Medical & Hospital Taxes	Property Tax	Natural Resources Taxes	Import Duties	Other Taxes	Total Taxes
5000	338	41	145	68	51	125	390	16	49	51	1275
5500	399	56	166	78	59	141	460	19	56	60	1493
6000	463	116	184	87	65	153	534	22	62	69	1755
6500	527	175	202	95	72	165	608	25	68	78	2017
7000	553	211	239	113	85	208	637	27	81	85	2236
7500	564	237	282	133	100	262	650	27	95	90	2440
8000	575	263	325	154	115	316	662	28	110	96	2644
8500	586	301	370	174	131	371	675	28	125	102	2862
9000	595	428	420	198	149	436	686	29	142	110	3193
9500	604	555	471	222	167	500	696	29	159	119	3523
10000	613	682	522	246	185	565	707	30	176	127	3853
10500	623	809	573	270	203	629	718	30	193	136	4183
11000	629	937	623	294	221	694	725	30	210	144	4507
11500	629	1065	673	318	238	759	725	30	227	150	4815
12000	629	1193	724	341	256	824	724	30	244	157	5123
12500	628	1322	774	365	274	889	724	30	261	163	5431
13000	628	1450	824	389	292	955	724	30	278	170	5739
13500	609	1571	868	410	307	1016	702	29	293	174	5979
14000	570	1683	905	427	321	1072	656	27	306	176	6142
14500	530	1795	943	445	334	1128	610	26	318	177	6305
15000	490	1907	980	462	347	1184	565	24	331	179	6468
15500	450	2019	1017	480	360	1240	519	22	343	181	6630
16000	410	2131	1054	498	373	1296	473	20	356	182	6793

TABLE A-17 continued

(Dollars per family)

Your Cash Income	Profits Tax	Income Tax	Sales Tax	Liquor, Tobacco, Amusement and Other Excise Taxes	Auto, Fuel $ Motor Vehicle Licence Taxes	Social Security, Pension, Medical & Hospital Taxes	Property Tax	Natural Resources Taxes	Import Duties	Other Taxes	Total Taxes
16500	391	2245	1092	515	387	1348	451	19	369	186	7003
17000	399	2363	1130	533	400	1396	460	19	381	191	7273
17500	407	2481	1167	551	413	1443	470	20	394	196	7543
18000	416	2599	1205	569	427	1491	478	20	407	202	7813
18500	424	2717	1243	586	440	1538	488	20	419	207	8083
19000	432	2835	1280	604	453	1586	498	21	432	212	8354
19500	440	2953	1318	622	467	1633	507	21	445	218	8624
20000	448	3071	1356	640	480	1681	516	22	458	223	8894
20500	456	3189	1393	658	493	1728	526	22	470	229	9164
21000	464	3307	1431	675	507	1776	535	22	483	234	9434
21500	474	3433	1469	693	520	1824	546	23	496	240	9719
22000	484	3562	1508	711	534	1872	558	23	509	247	10008
22500	494	3690	1546	730	547	1920	569	24	522	254	10296
23000	504	3819	1584	748	561	1968	581	24	535	261	10585
23500	514	3947	1623	766	575	2016	593	25	548	267	10873
24000	524	4076	1661	784	588	2064	604	25	561	274	11162
24500	534	4204	1699	802	602	2112	616	26	574	281	11450
25000	544	4333	1738	820	615	2160	627	26	587	288	11739
25500	555	4461	1776	838	629	2208	639	27	600	295	12027
26000	565	4590	1814	856	642	2256	651	27	613	301	12316
26500	575	4718	1853	874	656	2304	662	28	625	308	12604
27000	585	4847	1891	892	670	2352	674	28	638	315	12893
27500	653	4982	1930	911	683	2390	752	31	651	327	13310
28000	742	5120	1968	929	697	2423	856	36	664	340	13376
28500	832	5258	2007	947	711	2457	959	40	677	354	14242
29000	922	5396	2045	965	724	2490	1062	44	690	368	14708

Income											
29500	1012	5534	2084	983	738	2523	1166	49	703	381	15174
30000	1101	5672	2122	1002	752	2557	1269	53	717	395	15640
30500	1191	5810	2161	1020	765	2590	1373	57	730	408	16105
31000	1281	5948	2200	1038	779	2624	1476	62	743	422	16571
31500	1371	6086	2238	1056	792	2657	1580	66	756	436	17037
32000	1460	6224	2277	1074	806	2690	1683	70	769	449	17503
32500	1550	6362	2315	1093	820	2724	1786	75	782	463	17969
33000	1640	6500	2354	1111	833	2757	1890	79	795	476	18435
33500	1630	6646	2392	1129	847	2809	1878	78	808	485	18703
34000	1570	6796	2430	1147	861	2870	1809	76	820	492	18870
34500	1509	6946	2469	1165	874	2931	1740	73	833	499	19038
35000	1449	7096	2507	1183	888	2992	1670	70	846	505	19206
35500	1389	7246	2545	1201	901	3053	1601	67	859	512	19373
36000	1329	7396	2583	1219	915	3114	1531	64	872	518	19541
36500	1269	7546	2621	1237	928	3175	1462	61	885	525	19709
37000	1208	7696	2659	1255	942	3236	1393	58	898	532	19877
37500	1148	7846	2698	1273	955	3297	1323	55	911	538	20044
38000	1088	7996	2736	1291	969	3358	1254	52	924	545	20212
38500	1028	8146	2774	1309	982	3419	1185	49	936	552	20380
39000	968	8296	2812	1327	996	3480	1115	47	949	558	20547
39500	953	8436	2847	1343	1008	3528	1099	46	961	570	20791
40000	969	8569	2880	1359	1020	3567	1117	47	972	586	21085
40500	984	8703	2913	1374	1031	3607	1135	47	983	601	21379
41000	1000	8836	2945	1390	1043	3647	1152	48	994	617	21672
41500	1016	8969	2978	1405	1054	3687	1170	49	1005	632	21966
42000	1031	9103	3011	1421	1066	3726	1188	50	1016	648	22260
42500	1047	9236	3044	1436	1078	3766	1206	50	1027	663	22554
43000	1062	9370	3076	1452	1089	3806	1224	51	1039	679	22847
43500	1078	9503	3109	1467	1101	3845	1242	52	1050	694	23141
44000	1093	9636	3142	1483	1112	3885	1260	53	1061	710	23435
44500	1109	9770	3175	1498	1124	3925	1278	53	1072	725	23729
45000	1125	9903	3207	1513	1136	3965	1296	54	1083	741	24022

SCHEDULE A-17

1980 Detailed Tax Calculation for the Province of Nova Scotia

1. Profit tax = Your Cash Income x .025 _____
2. Income tax = Your Cash Income x .220 _____
3. Sales tax = Your Cash Income x .071 _____
4. Liquor, tobacco, amusement
   & other excise taxes = Your Cash Income x .034 _____
5. Auto, fuel & motor
   vehicle licence fees = Your Cash Income x .025 _____
6. Social security, pension,
   medical & hospital taxes = Your Cash Income x .088 _____
7. Property tax = Your Cash Income x .029 _____
8. Natural resources taxes = Your Cash Income x .001 _____
9. Import duties = Your Cash Income x .024 _____
10. Other taxes = Your Cash Income x .017 _____

Total taxes 1 + 2 + 3 + 4 + 5 + 6 + 7 + 8 + 9 + 10 = _____

TABLE A-18

1980 Tax Table for the Province of Ontario

(Dollars per family)

Your Cash Income	Profits Tax	Income Tax	Sales Tax	Liquor, Tobacco, Amusement and Other Excise Taxes	Auto, Fuel & Motor Vehicle Licence Taxes	Social Security, Pension, Medical & Hospital Taxes	Property Tax	Natural Resources Taxes	Import Duties	Other Taxes	Total Taxes
5000	406	34	160	39	36	647	406	21	35	107	1891
5500	457	42	188	46	42	765	456	24	41	122	2183
6000	458	91	228	56	51	939	457	24	50	136	2491
6500	459	141	269	66	60	1112	458	24	59	150	2799
7000	498	174	305	75	68	1121	497	26	70	164	2995
7500	563	196	337	83	75	1018	563	30	74	177	3114
8000	628	218	368	90	82	915	628	33	81	190	3234
8500	693	240	400	98	89	812	693	37	88	202	3353
9000	779	341	448	110	100	885	779	41	98	230	3812
9500	867	447	496	122	111	970	866	46	109	259	4292
10000	955	553	545	134	122	1054	954	50	120	287	4772
10500	1042	659	594	146	132	1138	1041	55	130	315	5252
11000	1122	765	642	158	143	1217	1121	59	141	342	5710
11500	1091	872	692	170	155	1229	1090	58	152	344	5853
12000	1061	978	742	182	166	1241	1060	56	163	345	5996
12500	1031	1085	793	195	177	1253	1030	55	174	347	6140
13000	1001	1192	843	207	188	1265	1000	53	185	348	6283
13500	982	1297	891	219	199	1275	981	52	196	351	6441
14000	1008	1390	931	229	208	1272	1007	53	205	360	6662
14500	1034	1483	971	239	217	1270	1033	55	214	368	6883
15000	1060	1577	1012	248	226	1267	1059	56	222	377	7104
15500	1086	1670	1052	258	235	1265	1085	57	231	385	7325
16000	1113	1763	1092	268	244	1262	1112	59	240	393	7546

TABLE A-18 continued

(Dollars per family)

Your Cash Income	Profits Tax	Income Tax	Sales Tax	Liquor, Tobacco, Amusement and Other Excise Taxes	Auto, Fuel & Motor Vehicle Licence Taxes	Social Security, Pension, Medical & Hospital Taxes	Property Tax	Natural Resources Taxes	Import Duties	Other Taxes	Total Taxes
16500	1132	1857	1133	278	253	1262	1131	60	249	401	7757
17000	1095	1956	1176	289	262	1285	1094	58	259	401	7874
17500	1058	2054	1219	299	272	1308	1057	56	268	401	7992
18000	1020	2152	1262	310	282	1331	1019	54	278	401	8109
18500	983	2251	1306	321	291	1354	982	52	287	401	8227
19000	945	2349	1349	331	301	1377	945	50	297	401	8345
19500	908	2447	1392	342	311	1400	907	48	306	401	8462
20000	871	2546	1435	352	320	1423	870	46	316	401	8580
20500	833	2644	1478	363	330	1446	833	44	325	401	8697
21000	796	2742	1522	374	340	1469	795	42	335	401	8815
21500	771	2844	1563	384	349	1497	770	41	344	403	8965
22000	768	2951	1601	393	357	1534	767	41	352	409	9173
22500	765	3058	1639	402	366	1571	764	40	360	415	9381
23000	762	3165	1677	412	374	1608	761	40	369	421	9589
23500	759	3272	1715	421	383	1646	758	40	377	427	9797
24000	756	3379	1753	430	391	1683	755	40	385	433	10006
24500	753	3486	1790	440	400	1720	752	40	394	439	10214
25000	750	3594	1828	449	408	1757	749	40	402	445	10422
25500	747	3701	1866	458	417	1794	747	40	410	451	10630
26000	744	3808	1904	468	425	1831	744	39	419	457	10838
26500	741	3915	1942	477	434	1868	741	39	427	463	11047
27000	738	4022	1980	486	442	1905	738	39	435	469	11255
27500	737	4130	2018	496	451	1943	736	39	444	475	11468
28000	740	4245	2057	505	459	1985	740	39	452	484	11705
28500	744	4360	2095	514	468	2026	743	39	461	492	11943
29000	747	4475	2133	524	476	2068	747	40	469	500	12180

29500	751	4590	2172	533	485	2110	750	40	478	509	12417
30000	755	4705	2210	543	493	2151	754	40	486	517	12655
30500	758	4820	2249	552	502	2193	758	40	494	525	12892
31000	762	4935	2287	562	511	2235	761	40	503	534	13130
31500	766	5050	2325	571	519	2276	765	40	511	542	13367
32000	769	5165	2364	580	528	2318	769	41	520	550	13604
32500	773	5280	2402	590	536	2360	772	41	528	559	13842
33000	777	5395	2441	599	545	2401	776	41	537	567	14079
33500	780	5510	2479	609	553	2443	780	41	545	575	14317
34000	824	5635	2519	618	562	2494	824	44	554	592	14666
34500	869	5760	2558	628	571	2545	869	46	562	608	15018
35000	914	5885	2598	638	580	2597	913	48	571	625	15370
35500	959	6010	2637	648	589	2648	958	51	580	642	15722
36000	1004	6135	2677	657	598	2699	1003	53	589	658	16073
36500	1049	6260	2717	667	606	2750	1048	55	597	675	16425
37000	1094	6385	2756	677	615	2801	1093	58	606	691	16777
37500	1139	6510	2796	686	624	2852	1138	60	615	708	17128
38000	1184	6635	2835	696	633	2904	1183	63	623	724	17480
38500	1229	6760	2875	706	642	2955	1227	65	632	741	17832
39000	1273	6885	2915	716	651	3006	1272	67	641	758	18184
39500	1318	7010	2954	725	659	3057	1317	70	650	774	18535
40000	1375	7124	2996	736	669	3086	1374	73	659	796	18887
40500	1436	7236	3037	746	678	3109	1434	76	668	820	19240
41000	1496	7347	3079	756	687	3132	1495	79	677	843	19592
41500	1556	7458	3121	766	697	3155	1555	82	686	867	19944
42000	1616	7569	3163	777	706	3178	1615	85	695	891	20296
42500	1677	7680	3205	787	715	3202	1675	89	705	914	20648
43000	1737	7791	3247	797	725	3225	1735	92	714	938	21001
43500	1797	7903	3289	808	734	3248	1796	95	723	961	21353
44000	1857	8014	3330	818	743	3271	1856	98	732	985	21705
44500	1918	8125	3372	828	753	3294	1916	101	741	1008	22057
45000	1978	8236	3414	838	762	3317	1976	105	751	1032	22409

Appendix

SCHEDULE A-18

1980 Detailed Tax Calculation for the Province of Ontario

1. Profit tax	= Your Cash Income x .044	
2. Income tax	= Your Cash Income x .183	
3. Sales tax	= Your Cash Income x .076	
4. Liquor, tobacco, amusement & other excise taxes	= Your Cash Income x .019	
5. Auto, fuel & motor vehicle licence fees	= Your Cash Income x .017	
6. Social security, pension, medical & hospital taxes	= Your Cash Income x .074	
7. Property tax	= Your Cash Income x .044	
8. Natural resources taxes	= Your Cash Income x .002	
9. Import duties	= Your Cash Income x .017	
10. Other taxes	= Your Cash Income x .023	

Total taxes   1 + 2 + 3 + 4 + 5 + 6 + 7 + 8 + 9 + 10   =

TABLE A-19

1980 Tax Table for the Province of Prince Edward Island

(Dollars per family)

Your Cash Income	Profits Tax	Income Tax	Sales Tax	Liquor, Tobacco, Amusement and Other Excise Taxes	Auto, Fuel & Motor Vehicle Licence Taxes	Social Security, Pension, Medical & Hospital Taxes	Property Tax	Natural Resources Taxes	Import Duties	Other Taxes	Total Taxes
5000	238	35	109	45	52	106	288	8	58	17	955
5500	265	72	115	47	55	109	321	9	61	17	1071
6000	289	120	118	48	57	107	350	10	62	15	1176
6500	309	157	137	56	66	131	374	10	72	14	1327
7000	322	178	178	73	86	189	390	11	94	16	1538
7500	335	199	220	90	106	247	406	11	116	17	1748
8000	349	222	261	107	126	305	422	12	138	19	1959
8500	348	325	297	122	143	358	422	12	157	20	2202
9000	348	428	333	136	160	411	422	12	176	20	2445
9500	348	532	368	151	177	464	421	12	195	21	2689
10000	347	635	404	166	195	517	421	12	213	22	2932
10500	346	739	437	179	210	565	419	12	231	23	3159
11000	342	843	465	190	224	607	415	11	245	25	3366
11500	339	947	492	202	237	649	411	11	260	26	3574
12000	336	1051	520	213	250	690	407	11	275	27	3782
12500	332	1156	548	225	264	732	403	11	289	29	3989
13000	332	1248	582	239	280	782	402	11	307	31	4213
13500	332	1339	616	253	296	833	402	11	325	32	4439
14000	332	1430	650	267	313	883	402	11	343	34	4666
14500	331	1521	685	281	329	934	401	11	362	36	4892
15000	331	1612	719	295	346	985	401	11	380	38	5118
15500	331	1704	752	308	362	1033	401	11	397	40	5339
16000	331	1800	775	318	373	1067	403	11	409	40	5529

TABLE A-19 continued

(Dollars per family)

Your Cash Income	Profits Tax	Income Tax	Sales Tax	Liquor, Tobacco, Amusement and Other Excise Taxes	Auto, Fuel & Motor Vehicle Licence Taxes	Social Security, Pension, Medical & Hospital Taxes	Property Tax	Natural Resources Taxes	Import Duties	Other Taxes	Total Taxes
16500	334	1896	798	327	384	1101	405	11	422	41	5719
17000	335	1992	822	337	395	1135	406	11	434	41	5910
17500	337	2088	845	347	407	1170	408	11	446	42	6100
18000	338	2184	869	356	418	1204	409	11	459	42	6291
18500	339	2280	892	366	429	1238	411	11	471	43	6481
19000	341	2375	916	376	441	1273	413	11	484	43	6672
19500	342	2471	939	385	452	1307	414	11	496	44	6862
20000	343	2568	963	395	463	1342	416	11	509	44	7054
20500	350	2672	996	408	479	1389	424	12	526	45	7302
21000	357	2776	1029	422	495	1436	433	12	543	46	7549
21500	364	2881	1062	435	511	1483	441	12	561	47	7796
22000	371	2985	1095	449	527	1529	449	12	578	48	8044
22500	378	3090	1127	462	542	1576	458	13	595	49	8291
23000	385	3194	1160	476	558	1623	466	13	613	50	8538
23500	391	3299	1193	489	574	1670	474	13	630	51	8785
24000	398	3403	1226	503	590	1717	483	13	647	52	9033
24500	405	3507	1259	516	606	1764	491	14	665	53	9280
25000	412	3612	1292	530	622	1811	499	14	682	54	9527
25500	419	3716	1325	543	637	1858	507	14	699	55	9775
26000	433	3825	1357	556	653	1902	525	14	717	58	10041
26500	452	3938	1389	570	668	1945	547	15	733	62	10319
27000	470	4050	1421	583	684	1988	570	16	750	66	10598
27500	489	4162	1453	596	699	2031	592	16	767	70	10876
28000	507	4274	1485	609	715	2074	615	17	784	74	11154
28500	526	4386	1517	622	730	2117	637	18	801	78	11433
29000	544	4498	1549	635	745	2160	660	18	818	82	11711

Income											
29500	563	4610	1581	648	761	2203	682	19	835	86	11989
30000	582	4722	1613	662	776	2246	705	19	852	90	12268
30500	600	4835	1645	675	792	2289	727	20	869	94	12546
31000	619	4947	1677	688	807	2332	750	21	886	98	12824
31500	644	5061	1707	700	821	2371	780	21	901	102	13109
32000	696	5183	1728	708	831	2389	843	23	912	105	13418
32500	748	5305	1748	717	841	2407	906	25	923	108	13727
33000	800	5426	1769	725	851	2425	969	27	934	111	14037
33500	852	5548	1789	734	861	2443	1032	28	945	114	14346
34000	904	5670	1809	742	871	2462	1095	30	955	117	14655
34500	956	5792	1830	750	880	2480	1157	32	966	120	14964
35000	1007	5914	1850	759	890	2498	1220	34	977	124	15273
35500	1059	6036	1871	767	900	2516	1283	35	988	127	15583
36000	1111	6158	1891	775	910	2535	1346	37	999	130	15892
36500	1163	6280	1912	784	920	2553	1409	39	1009	133	16201
37000	1215	6402	1932	792	930	2571	1472	40	1020	136	16510
37500	1229	6513	1957	803	942	2605	1489	41	1033	140	16752
38000	1232	6621	1984	813	954	2643	1493	41	1047	144	16974
38500	1235	6730	2010	824	967	2681	1497	41	1061	149	17196
39000	1239	6838	2037	835	980	2720	1500	41	1075	153	17418
39500	1242	6947	2063	846	993	2758	1504	41	1089	157	17640
40000	1245	7055	2090	857	1005	2796	1508	41	1103	161	17862
40500	1248	7163	2116	868	1018	2835	1512	42	1117	166	18085
41000	1251	7272	2142	878	1031	2873	1516	42	1131	170	18307
41500	1255	7380	2169	889	1044	2911	1520	42	1145	174	18529
42000	1258	7489	2195	900	1056	2950	1523	42	1159	178	18751
42500	1261	7597	2222	911	1069	2988	1527	42	1173	183	18973
43000	1264	7705	2248	922	1082	3026	1531	42	1187	187	19195
43500	1267	7814	2275	933	1095	3065	1535	42	1201	191	19417
44000	1270	7922	2301	944	1107	3103	1539	42	1215	196	19639
44500	1274	8031	2328	954	1120	3141	1543	42	1229	200	19862
45000	1277	8139	2354	965	1133	3179	1547	43	1243	204	20084

SCHEDULE A-19

**1980 Detailed Tax Calculation for the
Province of Prince Edward Island**

1. Profit tax	= Your Cash Income x .028	
2. Income tax	= Your Cash Income x .181	
3. Sales tax	= Your Cash Income x .052	
4. Liquor, tobacco, amusement & other excise taxes	= Your Cash Income x .022	
5. Auto, fuel & motor vehicle licence fees	= Your Cash Income x .025	
6. Social security, pension, medical & hospital taxes	= Your Cash Income x .071	
7. Property tax	= Your Cash Income x .034	
8. Natural resources taxes	= Your Cash Income x .001	
9. Import duties	= Your Cash Income x .028	
10. Other taxes	= Your Cash Income x .005	

Total taxes 1 + 2 + 3 + 4 + 5 + 6 + 7 + 8 + 9 + 10 =

TABLE A-20

1980 Tax Table for the Province of Quebec

Your Cash Income	Profits Tax	Income Tax	Sales Tax	Liquor, Tobacco, Amusement and Other Excise Taxes	Auto, Fuel & Motor Vehicle Licence Taxes	Social Security, Pension, Medical & Hospital Taxes	Property Tax	Natural Resources Taxes	Import Duties	Other Taxes	Total Taxes
						(Dollars per family)					
5000	292	42	129	43	43	83	293	23	33	132	1113
5500	350	74	156	52	53	100	351	28	40	162	1367
6000	424	134	191	64	64	123	426	33	49	202	1712
6500	496	191	225	75	76	145	498	39	58	238	2041
7000	552	217	250	83	84	161	553	44	64	240	2248
7500	607	244	275	92	92	178	609	48	70	242	2456
8000	662	270	300	100	101	194	664	52	77	245	2663
8500	711	358	340	113	114	225	713	56	87	268	2985
9000	755	486	392	131	132	266	757	60	101	305	3383
9500	799	614	443	148	149	308	801	63	114	342	3781
10000	843	743	495	165	166	350	845	66	127	379	4179
10500	887	871	546	182	184	391	890	70	140	416	4577
11000	940	1000	600	200	202	434	942	74	154	448	4993
11500	993	1130	654	218	220	476	996	78	168	478	5410
12000	1046	1259	707	236	238	518	1049	83	182	509	5827
12500	1100	1389	761	254	256	561	1103	87	195	540	6244
13000	1118	1514	810	270	272	604	1121	88	208	566	6572
13500	1017	1628	845	282	284	647	1020	80	217	576	6597
14000	917	1741	880	293	296	691	920	72	226	586	6621
14500	816	1854	915	305	307	735	819	64	235	596	6645
15000	716	1967	950	317	319	778	718	56	244	606	6670
15500	615	2080	985	328	331	822	617	48	253	616	6694
16000	550	2195	1023	341	344	864	552	43	262	629	6804

TABLE A-20 continued

(Dollars per family)

Your Cash Income	Profits Tax	Income Tax	Sales Tax	Liquor, Tobacco, Amusement and Other Excise Taxes	Auto, Fuel & Motor Vehicle Licence Taxes	Social Security, Pension, Medical & Hospital Taxes	Property Tax	Natural Resources Taxes	Import Duties	Other Taxes	Total Taxes
16500	547	2314	1066	355	358	904	548	43	274	650	7059
17000	544	2433	1109	370	373	944	545	43	285	670	7315
17500	540	2553	1152	384	387	983	542	43	296	691	7571
18000	537	2672	1196	398	402	1023	539	42	307	711	7826
18500	534	2791	1239	413	416	1063	535	42	318	731	8082
19000	531	2910	1282	427	431	1102	532	42	329	752	8337
19500	527	3029	1325	442	445	1142	529	42	340	772	8593
20000	524	3148	1368	456	460	1181	526	41	351	792	8849
20500	521	3267	1412	470	474	1221	522	41	362	813	9104
21000	542	3397	1448	483	487	1252	544	43	372	834	9401
21500	564	3527	1485	495	499	1283	565	44	381	855	9698
22000	585	3656	1522	507	511	1314	587	46	391	875	9995
22500	606	3786	1559	520	524	1345	608	48	400	896	10292
23000	628	3916	1596	532	536	1376	630	50	410	917	10589
23500	649	4046	1632	544	548	1407	651	51	419	938	10886
24000	671	4175	1669	556	561	1438	673	53	428	959	11183
24500	692	4305	1706	569	573	1468	694	55	438	980	11479
25000	713	4435	1743	581	586	1499	715	56	447	1001	11776
25500	735	4564	1780	593	598	1530	737	58	457	1021	12073
26000	756	4694	1816	605	610	1561	758	60	466	1042	12370
26500	772	4827	1854	618	623	1593	774	61	476	1064	12661
27000	773	4966	1894	631	636	1629	775	61	486	1087	12938
27500	774	5105	1933	644	650	1665	776	61	496	1110	13214
28000	775	5245	1973	657	663	1701	777	61	506	1133	13491
28500	776	5384	2012	671	676	1737	778	61	516	1156	13768
29000	777	5523	2052	684	689	1773	779	61	527	1179	14044

29500	778	5662	2091	697	703	1808	780	61	537	1203	14321
30000	779	5802	2131	710	716	1844	781	61	547	1226	14597
30500	780	5941	2171	723	729	1880	782	62	557	1249	14874
31000	781	6080	2210	737	743	1916	783	62	567	1272	15150
31500	782	6220	2250	750	756	1952	784	62	577	1295	15427
32000	783	6359	2289	763	769	1988	785	62	588	1318	15703
32500	790	6505	2327	775	782	2021	792	62	597	1341	15991
33000	801	6656	2362	787	794	2052	803	63	606	1363	16287
33500	812	6808	2398	799	806	2083	814	64	615	1385	16584
34000	823	6959	2433	811	817	2114	825	65	624	1408	16880
34500	834	7111	2469	823	829	2145	837	66	634	1430	17177
35000	845	7262	2504	835	841	2176	848	67	643	1452	17473
35500	857	7414	2540	846	853	2207	859	68	652	1475	17769
36000	868	7565	2575	858	865	2238	870	68	661	1497	18066
36500	879	7716	2611	870	877	2268	881	69	670	1519	18362
37000	890	7868	2646	882	889	2299	893	70	679	1542	18658
37500	901	8019	2682	894	901	2330	904	71	688	1564	18955
38000	912	8171	2717	906	913	2361	915	72	697	1586	19251
38500	952	8308	2755	918	926	2391	955	75	707	1617	19605
39000	998	8442	2794	931	939	2421	1001	79	717	1649	19969
39500	1043	8577	2832	944	951	2450	1046	82	727	1681	20333
40000	1088	8712	2870	957	964	2480	1091	86	737	1713	20697
40500	1133	8846	2909	969	977	2509	1136	89	747	1745	21061
41000	1178	8981	2947	982	990	2539	1182	93	756	1777	21425
41500	1224	9116	2985	995	1003	2568	1227	97	766	1809	21789
42000	1269	9250	3024	1008	1016	2598	1272	100	776	1841	22153
42500	1314	9385	3062	1021	1029	2627	1318	104	786	1873	22517
43000	1359	9520	3100	1033	1042	2657	1363	107	796	1905	22881
43500	1404	9654	3139	1046	1055	2686	1408	111	806	1937	23245
44000	1449	9789	3177	1059	1067	2716	1454	114	815	1969	23609
44500	1495	9924	3215	1072	1080	2745	1499	118	825	2001	23973
45000	1540	10058	3254	1084	1093	2774	1544	121	835	2033	24338

SCHEDULE A-20

1980 Detailed Tax Calculation for the Province of Quebec

1. Profit tax = Your Cash Income x .034 _____

2. Income tax = Your Cash Income x .224 _____

3. Sales tax = Your Cash Income x .072 _____

4. Liquor, tobacco, amusement & other excise taxes = Your Cash Income x .024 _____

5. Auto, fuel & motor vehicle licence fees = Your Cash Income x .024 _____

6. Social security, pension, medical & hospital taxes = Your Cash Income x .062 _____

7. Property tax = Your Cash Income x .034 _____

8. Natural resources taxes = Your Cash Income x .003 _____

9. Import duties = Your Cash Income x .019 _____

10. Other taxes = Your Cash Income x .045 _____

Total taxes   1 + 2 + 3 + 4 + 5 + 6 + 7 + 8 + 9 + 10   = _____

TABLE A-21

1980 Tax Table for the Province of Saskatchewan

Your Cash Income	Profits Tax	Income Tax	Sales Tax	Liquor, Tobacco, Amusement and Other Excise Taxes	Auto, Fuel & Motor Vehicle Licence Taxes	Social Security, Pension, Medical & Hospital Taxes	Property Tax	Natural Resources Taxes	Import Duties	Other Taxes	Total Taxes
					(Dollars per family)						
5000	563	37	142	84	67	348	580	1152	72	86	3131
5500	645	48	167	98	78	412	665	1321	85	100	3620
6000	651	103	179	106	84	416	671	1333	92	106	3741
6500	657	157	192	113	90	420	677	1345	98	111	3861
7000	682	192	209	124	98	423	702	1395	107	117	4049
7500	716	216	229	135	108	425	738	1466	117	123	4273
8000	751	240	249	147	117	427	773	1536	127	129	4496
8500	785	265	269	159	127	429	808	1606	138	135	4721
9000	792	382	305	180	144	480	815	1620	156	147	5020
9500	798	498	341	201	160	530	822	1634	174	159	5320
10000	805	615	377	223	177	581	829	1648	193	171	5619
10500	812	731	413	244	194	631	836	1662	211	183	5918
11000	814	848	447	264	210	680	839	1666	229	194	6190
11500	791	966	472	278	222	717	815	1620	241	200	6321
12000	769	1083	496	293	233	754	792	1573	254	205	6452
12500	746	1201	521	307	245	791	769	1527	266	210	6584
13000	724	1318	545	322	256	828	745	1481	279	216	6715
13500	718	1431	570	336	268	861	739	1469	291	222	6905
14000	749	1534	593	350	279	885	772	1533	303	230	7229
14500	781	1637	617	364	290	910	804	1598	315	238	7554
15000	812	1739	640	378	301	934	837	1663	327	247	7879
15500	844	1842	664	392	312	958	870	1728	339	255	8203
16000	876	1944	687	406	323	982	902	1792	352	263	8528

TABLE A-21 continued

Your Cash Income	Profits Tax	Income Tax	Sales Tax	Liquor, Tobacco, Amusement and Other Excise Taxes	Auto, Fuel & Motor Vehicle Licence Taxes	Social Security, Pension, Medical & Hospital Taxes	Property Tax	Natural Resources Taxes	Import Duties	Other Taxes	Total Taxes
					(Dollars per family)						
16500	901	2048	711	420	334	1007	929	1845	364	271	8830
17000	908	2157	735	434	346	1037	935	1858	376	277	9063
17500	914	2265	759	448	357	1066	942	1872	388	283	9295
18000	921	2373	783	462	368	1096	949	1885	401	289	9527
18500	928	2481	807	477	380	1126	956	1898	413	295	9760
19000	934	2589	831	491	391	1155	962	1912	425	301	9992
19500	941	2697	855	505	402	1185	969	1925	437	307	10224
20000	947	2805	879	519	414	1215	976	1938	450	313	10457
20500	954	2913	903	533	425	1244	982	1952	462	320	10689
21000	960	3022	927	548	436	1274	989	1965	474	326	10921
21500	972	3135	952	562	448	1308	1002	1990	487	333	11188
22000	989	3253	976	577	459	1345	1019	2025	499	341	11484
22500	1006	3370	1001	591	471	1382	1037	2060	512	349	11780
23000	1023	3488	1026	606	483	1419	1054	2094	525	358	12077
23500	1040	3606	1051	621	494	1457	1072	2129	537	366	12373
24000	1057	3724	1076	635	506	1494	1089	2164	550	374	12669
24500	1074	3841	1100	650	518	1531	1107	2199	563	382	12966
25000	1091	3959	1125	664	529	1568	1124	2234	575	391	13262
25500	1108	4077	1150	679	541	1605	1142	2269	588	399	13558
26000	1125	4195	1175	694	553	1643	1159	2303	601	407	13854
26500	1142	4312	1199	708	564	1680	1177	2338	613	415	14151
27000	1159	4430	1224	723	576	1717	1194	2373	626	424	14447
27500	1177	4551	1249	737	587	1754	1213	2410	639	432	14750
28000	1197	4678	1273	752	599	1790	1233	2449	651	441	15062
28500	1216	4804	1297	766	610	1826	1253	2488	663	450	15374
29000	1235	4931	1321	780	621	1863	1272	2528	676	459	15686

29500	1254	5057	1345	794	633	1899	1292	2567	688	468	15998
30000	1274	5184	1369	808	644	1935	1312	2607	700	477	16310
30500	1293	5310	1393	823	655	1971	1332	2646	712	486	16622
31000	1312	5436	1417	837	667	2008	1352	2685	725	495	16934
31500	1331	5563	1441	851	678	2044	1371	2725	737	505	17245
32000	1350	5689	1465	865	689	2080	1391	2764	749	514	17557
32500	1370	5816	1489	879	701	2116	1411	2803	762	523	17869
33000	1389	5942	1513	894	712	2153	1431	2843	774	532	18181
33500	1404	6072	1537	907	723	2193	1446	2873	786	541	18480
34000	1405	6209	1559	921	733	2243	1448	2876	797	551	18743
34500	1407	6346	1581	934	744	2294	1449	2880	809	561	19005
35000	1409	6484	1604	947	754	2344	1451	2883	820	571	19268
35500	1410	6621	1626	960	765	2394	1453	2887	832	581	19530
36000	1412	6759	1648	973	775	2445	1455	2890	843	591	19793
36500	1414	6896	1671	987	786	2495	1457	2894	855	601	20055
37000	1416	7034	1693	1000	797	2546	1458	2897	866	612	20317
37500	1417	7171	1715	1013	807	2596	1460	2901	877	622	20580
38000	1419	7309	1738	1026	818	2646	1462	2904	889	632	20842
38500	1421	7446	1760	1039	828	2697	1464	2908	900	642	21105
39000	1422	7583	1783	1053	839	2747	1465	2911	912	652	21367
39500	1432	7719	1804	1066	849	2793	1475	2931	923	662	21655
40000	1495	7841	1824	1077	858	2808	1540	3060	933	675	22112
40500	1558	7963	1843	1088	867	2823	1605	3190	943	688	22568
41000	1622	8086	1862	1100	876	2837	1670	3319	953	700	23025
41500	1685	8208	1882	1111	885	2852	1735	3448	962	713	23481
42000	1748	8330	1901	1123	894	2867	1800	3577	972	725	23938
42500	1811	8452	1920	1134	903	2882	1865	3706	982	738	24395
43000	1874	8575	1940	1145	913	2897	1930	3835	992	750	24851
43500	1937	8697	1959	1157	922	2912	1996	3964	1002	763	25308
44000	2000	8819	1978	1168	931	2926	2061	4094	1012	775	25764
44500	2063	8941	1998	1180	940	2941	2126	4223	1022	788	26221
45000	2126	9063	2017	1191	949	2956	2191	4352	1032	800	26677

SCHEDULE A-21

1980 Detailed Tax Calculation for the Province of Saskatchewan

1. Profit tax = Your Cash Income x .047 _____

2. Income tax = Your Cash Income x .201 _____

3. Sales tax = Your Cash Income x .045 _____

4. Liquor, tobacco, amusement
   & other excise taxes = Your Cash Income x .027 _____

5. Auto, fuel & motor
   vehicle licence fees = Your Cash Income x .021 _____

6. Social security, pension,
   medical & hospital taxes = Your Cash Income x .066 _____

7. Property tax = Your Cash Income x .049 _____

8. Natural resources taxes = Your Cash Income x .097 _____

9. Import duties = Your Cash Income x .023 _____

10. Other taxes = Your Cash Income x .018 _____

Total taxes $1 + 2 + 3 + 4 + 5 + 6 + 7 + 8 + 9 + 10$ = _____

TABLE A-22

1980 Tax Table for Canada

Your Cash Income	Profits Tax	Income Tax	Sales Tax	Liquor, Tobacco, Amusement and Other Excise Taxes	Auto, Fuel & Motor Vehicle Licence Taxes	Social Security, Pension, Medical & Hospital Taxes	Property Tax	Natural Resources Taxes	Import Duties	Other Taxes	Total Taxes
					(Dollars per family)						
5000	439	37	138	47	39	399	386	293	40	96	1915
5500	497	53	163	55	46	475	437	333	47	113	2218
6000	546	108	194	66	55	548	474	385	57	130	2562
6500	596	162	226	77	64	621	511	438	66	146	2906
7000	669	192	253	86	72	602	568	497	74	157	3170
7500	748	217	280	95	80	560	630	558	82	169	3415
8000	826	241	306	105	87	519	691	618	90	176	3660
8500	895	286	335	115	96	498	748	666	99	188	3927
9000	929	403	376	131	108	552	786	666	112	207	4271
9500	963	519	416	147	121	606	824	667	126	227	4615
10000	997	636	456	163	133	659	862	667	139	246	4959
10500	1031	753	497	178	145	713	900	667	152	266	5304
11000	1053	870	540	193	158	760	926	663	165	282	5610
11500	1058	985	586	208	171	799	934	651	177	295	5864
12000	1063	1101	633	222	184	838	942	639	189	308	6118
12500	1067	1216	679	236	196	876	950	627	202	321	6372
13000	1072	1332	726	250	209	915	958	616	214	334	6626
13500	1070	1440	765	263	221	945	955	617	224	345	6845
14000	1062	1543	801	275	231	968	945	627	234	355	7041
14500	1055	1646	836	286	241	992	935	637	244	364	7238
15000	1047	1749	872	298	251	1016	925	648	254	374	7434
15500	1040	1852	907	310	261	1039	915	658	264	384	7631
16000	1033	1955	943	322	271	1063	905	668	274	393	7827

TABLE A-22 continued

Your Cash Income	Profits Tax	Income Tax	Sales Tax	Liquor, Tobacco, Amusement and Other Excise Taxes	Auto, Fuel & Motor Vehicle Licence Taxes	Social Security, Pension, Medical & Hospital Taxes	Property Tax	Natural Resources Taxes	Import Duties	Other Taxes	Total Taxes
				(Dollars per family)							
16500	1019	2059	980	333	281	1092	890	670	284	401	8011
17000	1003	2164	1019	345	291	1124	873	668	294	408	8188
17500	986	2268	1057	356	301	1156	855	666	304	414	8365
18000	970	2372	1096	368	311	1188	838	664	315	421	8542
18500	953	2477	1135	380	321	1220	820	662	325	427	8719
19000	936	2581	1173	391	331	1252	802	660	335	434	8896
19500	920	2685	1212	403	341	1284	785	658	345	440	9073
20000	903	2790	1251	414	351	1316	767	656	355	447	9250
20500	887	2894	1289	426	361	1348	750	653	365	454	9427
21000	870	2998	1328	438	371	1380	732	651	375	460	9604
21500	874	3113	1363	448	381	1415	737	650	384	470	9835
22000	880	3229	1397	459	390	1450	743	648	393	481	10071
22500	886	3345	1432	469	399	1485	749	647	403	491	10306
23000	892	3460	1467	480	408	1520	756	645	412	502	10541
23500	898	3576	1501	490	418	1555	762	644	421	512	10776
24000	903	3692	1536	501	427	1590	768	642	430	523	11012
24500	909	3807	1571	511	436	1625	775	641	439	533	11247
25000	915	3923	1606	522	445	1660	781	639	448	544	11482
25500	921	4039	1640	532	455	1695	788	638	457	554	11718
26000	927	4154	1675	543	464	1730	794	636	466	564	11953
26500	933	4270	1710	553	473	1765	800	635	475	575	12188
27000	939	4386	1744	564	482	1800	807	633	484	585	12423
27500	960	4511	1777	575	491	1837	819	664	494	598	12726
28000	983	4636	1810	586	500	1875	832	698	503	610	13035
28500	1005	4762	1843	597	509	1914	845	732	513	623	13343
29000	1028	4888	1875	609	518	1952	858	766	522	636	13652

13961	648	532	800	871	1990	526	620	1908	5014	1051	29500
14269	661	541	834	885	2028	535	631	1941	5139	1074	30000
14578	674	551	868	898	2066	544	642	1973	5265	1096	30500
14887	686	560	902	911	2104	553	654	2006	5391	1119	31000
15196	699	570	936	924	2142	562	665	2039	5517	1142	31500
15504	712	580	970	937	2180	571	676	2071	5642	1165	32000
15813	724	589	1004	950	2219	580	687	2104	5768	1188	32500
16122	737	599	1038	963	2257	588	698	2137	5894	1210	33000
16431	753	608	1048	984	2297	598	709	2171	6029	1235	33500
16740	769	617	1055	1006	2338	607	719	2205	6164	1259	34000
17049	786	626	1061	1028	2378	616	730	2239	6300	1283	34500
17358	803	635	1068	1050	2419	625	740	2273	6436	1308	35000
17667	819	644	1075	1073	2460	634	751	2308	6572	1332	35500
17976	836	653	1082	1095	2500	644	761	2342	6708	1357	36000
18285	852	662	1088	1117	2541	653	772	2376	6844	1381	36500
18594	869	671	1095	1139	2581	662	782	2410	6980	1405	37000
18903	885	680	1102	1161	2622	671	793	2444	7116	1430	37500
19212	902	689	1108	1183	2663	680	803	2478	7252	1454	38000
19521	918	698	1115	1205	2703	690	813	2513	7387	1479	38500
19830	935	707	1122	1227	2744	699	824	2547	7523	1503	39000
20194	954	716	1151	1278	2771	707	834	2582	7641	1559	39500
20565	973	725	1182	1332	2796	716	844	2618	7757	1620	40000
20935	993	734	1214	1387	2821	725	854	2654	7873	1681	40500
21306	1013	743	1246	1441	2846	733	865	2689	7988	1741	41000
21677	1032	752	1278	1496	2871	742	875	2725	8104	1802	41500
22047	1052	761	1309	1550	2897	750	885	2761	8220	1862	42000
22418	1072	770	1341	1604	2922	759	895	2797	8336	1923	42500
22789	1091	779	1373	1659	2947	767	905	2832	8451	1983	43000
23159	1111	788	1405	1713	2972	776	915	2868	8567	2044	43500
23530	1130	797	1436	1768	2997	785	926	2904	8683	2104	44000
23901	1150	806	1468	1822	3022	793	936	2939	8799	2165	44500
24271	1170	815	1500	1876	3048	802	946	2975	8914	2226	45000

SCHEDULE A-22

1980 Detailed Tax Calculation for Canada

1. Profit tax = Your Cash Income x .050 _____

2. Income tax = Your Cash Income x .198 _____

3. Sales tax = Your Cash Income x .066 _____

4. Liquor, tobacco, amusement
   & other excise taxes = Your Cash Income x .021 _____

5. Auto, fuel & motor
   vehicle licence fees = Your Cash Income x .018 _____

6. Social security, pension,
   medical & hospital taxes = Your Cash Income x .068 _____

7. Property tax = Your Cash Income x .042 _____

8. Natural resources taxes = Your Cash Income x .033 _____

9. Import duties = Your Cash Income x .018 _____

10. Other taxes = Your Cash Income x .026 _____

Total taxes   1 + 2 + 3 + 4 + 5 + 6 + 7 + 8 + 9 + 10 _____

Notes

Preface

1   From conversations between one of the authors and Michael Parkin of the University of Western Ontario in May, 1979, in connection with a Canadian Broadcasting Corporation program on taxation.

Chapter 1

1   A survey of the evolution of the Canadian tax system with emphasis on the sharing of tax revenues between the provinces and the federal government can be found in Perrin Lewis' chapter, "The Tangled Tale of Taxes and Transfers," in M. Walker (editor), *Canadian Confederation at the Crossroads,* the Fraser Institute, 1979.

2   Douglas Hartle, "An Open Letter to Allen Lambert...," *The Financial Post,* Feb. 11, 1978. Mr. Hartle was a senior civil servant in the federal Treasury Board during the latter period of the income tax explosion.

3   For a complete discussion of oil pricing and taxation, see G.C. Watkins and M.A. Walker (editors), *Oil in the Seventies,* the Fraser Institute, 1977.

4   Brian L. Scarfe and Bruce W. Wilkinson, "The New Energy Agreement: An Economic Perspective," *Focus,* The Fraser Institute, February 1982.

5   A documentation of these developments can be found in Perrin Lewis, op. cit.

6   H.F. Campbell, "An Input-Output Analysis of the Commodity Structure of Indirect Taxes in Canada," *The Canadian Journal of Economics,* August 1975, p. 433.

7   This particular distinction is due to the work of E.K. Browning and W.R. Johnson of the University of Virginia who have recently completed a study of the burden of taxation in the United States.

This study, *The Distribution of the Tax Burden* by Edgar K. Browning and William R. Johnson, 1979, has been published by the American Enterprise Institute.

8   These studies, published in 1976 and 1977 respectively, were: *How Much Tax Do You Really Pay?*, M. Walker (editor), and *Income and Taxation in Canada 1961-1975*, S.C. Pipes and S. Star, the Fraser Institute.

9   E.K. Browning and William R. Johnson, *The Distribution of the Tax Burden*, American Enterprise Institute, 1979.

10 R.J. Wonnacott and Paul Wonnacott, *Free Trade Between the United States and Canada*, (Cambridge, Mass.: Harvard University Press, 1967), p. 299.

Chapter 2

1   K. Marx and Friedrich Engels, *Manifesto of the Communist Party*, 1848.

2   W.I. Gillespie, *In Search of Robin Hood*, C.D. Howe Research Institute, Montreal, 1978.

Chapter 3

1   Statistics Canada, *System of National Accounts, National Income and Expenditure Accounts*, Catalogue No. 13-201, Supply and Services Canada.

Chapter 4

1   Don McGillivray, "An Over-Simplified Look at our Complicated Taxes," *Financial Times of Canada*, November 8, 1976.

Glossary

Some of the Book's Principal Terms, Measures, and Concepts

About Indices

Index: a method of measuring the percentage change from a base year of a certain item, such as the price, volume or value of food or the dollar amount of taxes. In order to construct an Index, the price, volume or value of the particular item being indexed in each year is divided by the price, volume or value of that item in the base year; it is then multiplied by 100. An Index has a value of 100 in the base year; in this book the base year chosen is 1961.

Consumer Price Index: measures the percentage change from a base year in the cost of purchasing a constant "basket" of goods and services representing the purchases by a particular population group in a specified time period. The Consumer Price Index or CPI, as it is often called, reflects price movements of some 300 items. The CPI is calculated monthly by Statistics Canada (see below).

Consumer Tax Index: measures the percentage change from a base year in the average Canadian family's tax bill. The Consumer Tax Index or CTI is composed of Federal, Provincial, and Municipal taxes. The CTI, calculated by the Fraser Institute, was introduced for the first time in Edition One, *How Much Tax Do You Really Pay?*

Balanced Budget Tax Index: is the same as the Consumer Tax Index except that included in the calculation is the amount of tax that would have to be raised if governments did not issue debt and were in fact balancing their budgets. This index was introduced by the Fraser Institute for the first time in Edition Two, *Tax Facts.*

Some Statistical Terms

Statistics Canada: is Canada's official statistical agency which is often referred to as "StatCan". Statistics Canada provided much of the published and unpublished data for this book. For a detailed listing of these sources, see the Bibliography.

Average Canadian Family: represents a family that had average income in a particular year. The averages were constructed from Statistics Canada's expenditure surveys, details of which appear in the Bibliography.

Family Expenditure Survey: refers to the Statistics Canada surveys which show patterns of family expenditure for Canada by selected characteristics such as urban and/or rural area, family type, life cycle, income, age of head, tenure, occupation of head, education of head, country of origin and, if applicable, immigrant arrival year. The tables in these surveys which were integral to this book were those entitled, "Detailed Average Expenditure by Family Income for All Families and Unattached Individuals." From these tables it was possible to look at the spending patterns of the average family in each income class.

Family: refers to a group of persons dependent upon a common or pooled income for their major expenditure items and living in the same dwelling. The term also applies to a financially independent unattached individual living alone.

Shelter Expenditure: is included as one of the selected expenditure items in this book. It refers to expenditures on rented or owned living quarters, on repairs to these quarters; on mortgage interest and on other housing, such as vacation homes, lodging at university or at remote work locations. It also includes expenditures on water and heating fuel.

Income Concepts Used in the Book

Cash Income: is the income that a family would report when completing a government survey, such as the Family Expenditure Survey or the Census form. It includes income that one receives regularly, such as salary or wage income (before tax) and payments from government such as family allowances.

Full Cash Income: is cash income plus the extra income that is often omitted when a family speaks of its income. Items that are often excluded from cash income include bond or bank interest and dividend income.

Income from Government: is income that a family receives as payment *from* the government, whereas taxes are payments *to* the government. Therefore, income from the government can be considered a "negative tax". It is often referred to as a *transfer payment*. It includes such items as family allowance payments, old age security payments, veterans' grants, etc.

Hidden Income: is income that a family receives but probably does not consider to be part of its income. Hidden income is largely made up of employer contributions to pension plans, medical premiums, and insurance plans. Another example is imputed non-farm rent. (For a more complete discussion of imputed non-farm rent see the Fraser Institute publication *Rent Control — A Popular Paradox,* p. 33).

Hidden Purchasing Power Loss: the prices of articles that the family buys are higher by the amount of hidden taxes which are paid to government by an intermediary and not at the point of final sale. For example, sales taxes paid by the manufacturer are typically added to the price charged to the wholesaler or retailer and are accordingly built into the final sales price but not called a tax. Therefore, the consumer actually loses purchasing power by the amount of these taxes. In this book the purchasing power loss has been given back to the family as one of the components of total income before tax.

Total Income Before Tax: is the term used in this book to designate the amount of income the family would have received before paying tax. It is composed of full cash income which includes income from government (transfer payments), hidden income, and hidden purchasing power loss.

Deciles: all families were lined up according to total income before tax from lowest to highest and then divided into ten groups, i.e. the first decile contains the first 10 per cent of families etc.

Transfer Payments: see "Income from Government" in this section.

About Taxes

Tax Burden: is the means of determining who ultimately pays tax and is synonymous with the term "tax incidence." Tax burden is measured by the decline in real purchasing power that results from the imposition of a tax.

Balanced Budget Tax Rate: is the tax rate that Canadians would face if governments had to balance their budgets and finance all expenditures from current tax revenue instead of issuing debt.

Deferred Taxation: the debt incurred by the various levels of government to finance the expenditures that cannot be met by current tax revenue is, in effect, deferred taxation because the debts and interest on them must ultimately be paid out of future tax revenue.

Direct Taxes: are taxes which are paid directly by the family. Examples of direct taxes are the personal income tax and provincial retail sales taxes. They are often referred to as explicit taxes.

Hidden Taxes: are taxes that are concealed in the price of articles that one buys. Hidden taxes are also referred to as implicit taxes. The most well-known form of the hidden tax is the indirect tax. Examples of hidden taxes are the tobacco tax, manufacturers' sales taxes and import duties.

Social Security Taxes: are composed of both federal and provincial taxes. The federal category includes employer and employee contributions to Public Service Pensions and to Unemployment Insurance. Provincial Social Security taxes include employer and employee contributions to Public Service Pensions, employer and employee contributions to Workers' Compensation and Industrial Employees' Vacations. Also included in this category as taxes are payments to the Canada and Quebec Pension Plans and Medical and Hospital Insurance Premiums.

Corporate Profits Tax: is the tax paid on the profits of a corporation.

Progressive, Proportional and Regressive Taxation: these are terms which refer to the proportionality of taxes to income. A tax is called *proportional* if it takes the same friction of income from low income people as it does from high income people. (Unemployment Insurance payments and Canada Pension payments up to the maximum earnings level are examples of proportional taxes). A *progressive tax* is one that takes a greater proportion of income from high income people than from those with low incomes (income tax, for example). A *regressive tax* is one that takes a greater proportion of income from low income people than it does from high income people (sales tax, for example).

Negative Tax: see "Income from Government" in the previous section.

Taxing Powers Under the Constitution of Canada: the general scheme of taxation in the British North America Act might be summarized in this way:
1. the federal government is given an unlimited power to tax.
2. the provinces are also given what amounts to an unlimited power to tax "within the province", that is to say an unlimited power to tax persons within their jurisdiction and to impose taxes in respect of property located and income earned within the province. (They may not, however, levy indirect taxes.) But their taxing powers are framed in such a way as to preclude them from imposing taxes which would have the effect of creating barriers to interprovincial trade, and generally from taxing persons and property outside the province.

Bibliography

Selected Sources

Bird, Richard M., *Growth of Government Spending in Canada*, Canadian Tax Foundation, July 1970.

Browning, Edgar K., "The Burden of Taxation," *Journal of Political Economy*, Volume 86, Number 4, August 1978.

Browning, Edgar K. and William R. Johnson, *The Distribution of the Tax Burden*, American Enterprise Institute, 1979.

Campbell, Harry F., "An Input-Output Analysis of the Commodity Structure of Indirect Taxes in Canada," *The Canadian Journal of Economics*, August 1975, p. 433.

Canadian Tax Foundation, *The National Finances — An Analysis of the Revenues and Expenditures of the Government of Canada*, 1980-81, Canadian Tax Foundation, 1981.

_____, *The National Finances — An Analysis of the Revenues and Expenditures of the Government of Canada*, 1978-79, Canadian Tax Foundation, 1979.

_____, *The National Finances — An Analysis of the Revenues and Expenditures of the Government of Canada*, 1975-76, Canadian Tax Foundation, 1976.

_____, *The National Finances — An Analysis of the Revenues and Expenditures of the Government of Canada*, 1974-75, Canadian Tax Foundation, 1975.

_____, *Provincial and Municipal Finances*, 1979, Canadian Tax Foundation, 1979.

_____, *Provincial and Municipal Finances*, 1977, Canadian Tax Foundation, 1977.

_____, *Provincial and Municipal Finances*, 1975, Canadian Tax Foundation, 1975.

Dodge, David A., "Impact of Tax, Transfer and Expenditure Policies of

Government on the Distribution of Personal Incomes in Canada."
The Review of Income and Wealth, Series 21, Number 1, March
1975. pp. 1-52.

Gillespie, W. Irwin, *Incidence of Taxes and Public Expenditures in the
Canadian Economy*, (Studies of the Royal Commission on Taxation.
Number 2), 1966.

_____, *In Search of Robin Hood*, C.D. Howe Research Institute, 1978.

Goffman, Irving J., *The Burden of Canadian Taxation*, (Tax Paper
Number 29), Canadian Tax Foundation, July 1972.

Marx, Karl and Friedrich Engels, *Manifesto of the Communist Party*,
1848.

Maslove, Allan M., *The Pattern of Taxation in Canada*, Economic
Council of Canada, December 1972.

Meerman, Jacob P., "The Definition of Income in Studies of Budget
Incidence and Income Distribution," *Review of Income and Wealth*,
Series 20, Number 4, December 1974, pp. 512-22.

Musgrave, Richard A., and Peggy B. Musgrave, *Public Finance in
Theory and Practice*, McGraw-Hill, Inc., 1973.

Pechman, Joseph A., and Benjamin A. Okner, *Who Bears the Tax
Burden?* (Studies of Government Finance), The Brookings Institu-
tion, 1974.

Pipes, Sally C., and Michael A. Walker, *Tax Facts*, the Fraser Institute,
1979.

Star, Spencer and Sally C. Pipes, *Income and Taxation in Canada 1961-
1975*, the Fraser Institute, 1977.

Walker, Michael, ed., Thomas Courchene, Perrin Lewis, Pierre Lortie, et
al., *Canadian Confederation at the Crossroads: The Search for a
Federal-Provincial Balance*, the Fraser Institute, 1979.

Walker, Michael, ed., *How Much Tax Do You Really Pay?*, the Fraser
Institute, 1976.

Walker, Michael, ed., David Laidler, Michael Parkin, Jackson Grayson,
et al., *The Illusion of Wage and Price Control*, the Fraser Institute,
1976.

Walker, Michael and G. Campbell Watkins, editors, *Oil in the Seventies*,
the Fraser Institute, 1977.

Wonnacott, Ronald J. and P. Wonnacott, *Free Trade Between the United
States and Canada*, Harvard University Press, 1967.

Government Sources

Bank of Canada Review, Monthly.

Revenue Canada, Taxation, *Taxation Statistics, 1980 Edition, Analyzing the Returns of Individuals for the 1978 Taxation Year and Miscellaneous Statistics.*

———, *Taxation Statistics, 1978 Edition, Analyzing the Returns of Individuals for the 1976 Taxation Year and Miscellaneous Statistics.*

———, *Taxation Statistics, 1976 Edition, Analyzing the Returns of Individuals for the 1974 Taxation Year and Miscellaneous Statistics.*

———, *Taxation Statistics, 1974 Edition, Analyzing the Returns of Individuals for the 1972 Taxation Year and Miscellaneous Statistics.*

———, *Taxation Statistics, 1973 Edition, Analyzing the Returns of Individuals for the 1971 Taxation Year and Miscellaneous Statistics.*

———, *Taxation Statistics, 1971 Edition, Analyzing the Returns of Individuals for the 1969 Taxation Year and Miscellaneous Statistics.*

———, *Taxation Statistics, 1970 Edition, Analyzing the Returns of Individuals for the 1968 Taxation Year and Miscellaneous Statistics.*

———, *Taxation Statistics, 1963 Edition, Analyzing the Returns of Individuals for the 1961 Taxation Year.* *

———, *Taxation Statistics, 1962 Edition, analyzing the Returns of Individuals for the 1960 Taxation Year.* *

Statistics Canada, *Canada Year Book,* 1978, Supply and Services Canada, Ottawa.

———, *Perspective Canada — A Compendium of Social Statistics.* Supply and Services Canada, Ottawa.

———, *Canadian Statistical Review,* Catalogue No. 11-003 E. Monthly, Supply and Services Canada, Ottawa.

———, *System of National Accounts, National Income and Expenditure Accounts, Fourth Quarter and Preliminary Annual, 1980,* Catalogue No. 13-001, Supply and Services Canada, Ottawa.

———, *System of National Accounts, National Income and Expenditure Accounts, Fourth Quarter and Preliminary Annual, 1978,* Catalogue No. 13-001, Supply and Services Canada, Ottawa.

———, *System of National Accounts, National Income and Expenditure Accounts, Fourth Quarter and Preliminary Annual, 1976,* Catalogue No. 13-001, Supply and Services Canada, Ottawa.

———, *System of National Accounts, National Income and Expenditure Accounts, Fourth Quarter and Preliminary Annual, 1974,* Catalogue No. 13-001, Information Canada, Ottawa.

_____, *System of National Accounts, National Income and Expendi-ture Accounts, Fourth Quarter and Preliminary Annual, 1972, Cata-logue No. 13-001, Information Canada, Ottawa.*

_____, *System of National Accounts, National Income and Expendi-ture Accounts, Fourth Quarter and Preliminary Annual, 1971,* Cata-logue No. 13-001, Information Canada, Ottawa.

_____, *System of National Accounts, Financial Flow Accounts, Quar-terly, 1978,* Catalogue No. 13-002, Supply and Services Canada, Ottawa.

_____, *System of National Accounts, Financial Flow Accounts, Quar-terly, 1977,* Catalogue No. 13-002, Supply and Services Canada, Ottawa.

_____, *National Accounts, Income and Expenditure, 1962,* Catalogue No. 13-201, Information Canada, Ottawa.**

_____, *System of National Accounts. Provincial Economic Accounts. Experimental Data, 1963 to 1980,* Catalogue No. 13-213, Supply and Services Canada, Ottawa.

_____, *Income Distributions by Size in Canada, 1978,* Catalogue No. 13-207, Supply and Services Canada, Ottawa.

_____, *Income Distributions by Size in Canada, 1980,* Catalogue No. 13-207, Supply and Services Canada, Ottawa.

_____, *Income Distributions by Size in Canada, 1976,* Catalogue No. 13-207, Supply and Services Canada, Ottawa.

_____, *Income Distributions by Size in Canada, 1974,* Catalogue No. 13-207, Information Canada, Ottawa.

_____, *Income Distributions by Size in Canada, 1972,* Catalogue No. 13-207, Information Canada, Ottawa.

_____, *Distribution of Non-Farm Incomes in Canada by Size, 1961,* Catalogue No. 13-521, Information Canada, Ottawa.**

_____, *Income Distributions by Size in Canada, 1969,* Catalogue No. 13-544, Information Canada, Ottawa.

_____, *Farm Net Income, 1978,* Catalogue No. 21-202, Supply and Services Canada, Ottawa.

_____, *Prices and Price Indices,* Catalogue No. 62-001, Monthly, Sup-ply and Services Canada, Ottawa.

_____, *Urban Family Expenditure, 1962,* Catalogue No. 62-525, Infor-mation Canada, Ottawa.**

_____, *Family Expenditure in Canada, Volume 1, All Canada, 1969,* Catalogue No. 62-535, Information Canada, Ottawa.

_____, *Family Expenditure in Canada, Volume 3, Major Urban Cen-tres, 1969,* Catalogue No. 62-537, Information Canada, Ottawa.

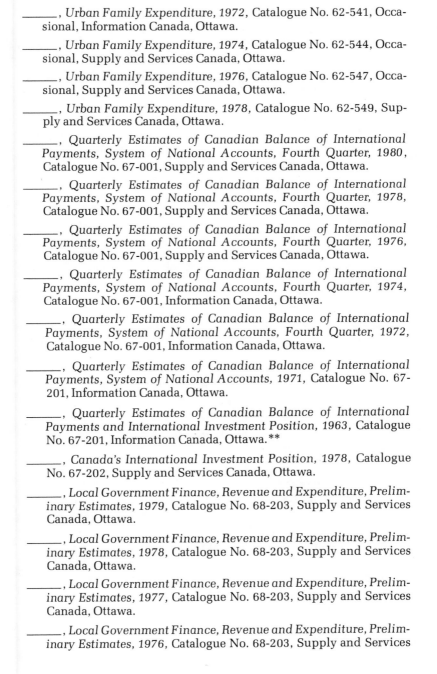

_____, *Urban Family Expenditure, 1972*, Catalogue No. 62-541, Occasional, Information Canada, Ottawa.

_____, *Urban Family Expenditure, 1974*, Catalogue No. 62-544, Occasional, Supply and Services Canada, Ottawa.

_____, *Urban Family Expenditure, 1976*, Catalogue No. 62-547, Occasional, Supply and Services Canada, Ottawa.

_____, *Urban Family Expenditure, 1978*, Catalogue No. 62-549, Supply and Services Canada, Ottawa.

_____, *Quarterly Estimates of Canadian Balance of International Payments, System of National Accounts, Fourth Quarter, 1980*, Catalogue No. 67-001, Supply and Services Canada, Ottawa.

_____, *Quarterly Estimates of Canadian Balance of International Payments, System of National Accounts, Fourth Quarter, 1978*, Catalogue No. 67-001, Supply and Services Canada, Ottawa.

_____, *Quarterly Estimates of Canadian Balance of International Payments, System of National Accounts, Fourth Quarter, 1976*, Catalogue No. 67-001, Supply and Services Canada, Ottawa.

_____, *Quarterly Estimates of Canadian Balance of International Payments, System of National Accounts, Fourth Quarter, 1974*, Catalogue No. 67-001, Information Canada, Ottawa.

_____, *Quarterly Estimates of Canadian Balance of International Payments, System of National Accounts, Fourth Quarter, 1972*, Catalogue No. 67-001, Information Canada, Ottawa.

_____, *Quarterly Estimates of Canadian Balance of International Payments, System of National Accounts, 1971*, Catalogue No. 67-201, Information Canada, Ottawa.

_____, *Quarterly Estimates of Canadian Balance of International Payments and International Investment Position, 1963*, Catalogue No. 67-201, Information Canada, Ottawa.**

_____, *Canada's International Investment Position, 1978*, Catalogue No. 67-202, Supply and Services Canada, Ottawa.

_____, *Local Government Finance, Revenue and Expenditure, Preliminary Estimates, 1979*, Catalogue No. 68-203, Supply and Services Canada, Ottawa.

_____, *Local Government Finance, Revenue and Expenditure, Preliminary Estimates, 1978*, Catalogue No. 68-203, Supply and Services Canada, Ottawa.

_____, *Local Government Finance, Revenue and Expenditure, Preliminary Estimates, 1977*, Catalogue No. 68-203, Supply and Services Canada, Ottawa.

_____, *Local Government Finance, Revenue and Expenditure, Preliminary Estimates, 1976*, Catalogue No. 68-203, Supply and Services

Canada, Ottawa.

_____, *Local Government Finance, Revenue and Expenditure, Preliminary Estimates, 1975*, Catalogue No. 68-203, Supply and Services Canada, Ottawa.

_____, *Local Government Finance, Revenue and Expenditure, Preliminary Estimates, 1974*, Catalogue No. 68-203, Information Canada, Ottawa.

_____, *Local Government Finance, Revenue and Expenditure, Preliminary Estimates, 1973*, Catalogue No. 68-203, Information Canada, Ottawa.

_____, *Local Government Finance, Revenue and Expenditure, Preliminary Estimates, 1972*, Catalogue No. 68-203, Information Canada, Ottawa.

_____, *Local Government Finance, Revenue and Expenditure, Preliminary Estimates, 1971*, Catalogue No. 68-203, Information Canada, Ottawa.

_____, *Local Government Finance, Revenue and Expenditure, Preliminary Estimates, 1969*, Catalogue No. 68-203, Information Canada, Ottawa.

_____, *Local Government Finance, Revenue and Expenditure, Preliminary Estimates, 1968*, Catalogue No. 68-203, Information Canada, Ottawa.

_____, *Local Government Finance, Revenue and Expenditure, Preliminary Estimates, 1961*, Catalogue No. 68-203, Information Canada, Ottawa.**

_____, *Local Government Finance, Revenue and Expenditure, Preliminary Estimates, 1960*, Catalogue No. 68-203, Information Canada, Ottawa.**

_____, *Provincial Government Finance, Revenue and Expenditure, 1979*, Catalogue No. 68-207, Supply and Services Canada, Ottawa.

_____, *Provincial Government Finance, Revenue and Expenditure, 1978*, Catalogue No. 68-207, Supply and Services Canada, Ottawa.

_____, *Provincial Government Finance, Revenue and Expenditure, 1977*, Catalogue No. 68-207, Supply and Services Canada, Ottawa.

_____, *Provincial Government Finance, Revenue and Expenditure, 1976*, Catalogue No. 68-207, Supply and Services Canada, Ottawa.

_____, *Provincial Government Finance, Revenue and Expenditure, 1975*, Catalogue No. 68-207, Information Canada, Ottawa.

_____, *Provincial Government Finance, Revenue and Expenditure, 1974*, Catalogue No. 68-207, Information Canada, Ottawa.

_____, *Provincial Government Finance, Revenue and Expenditure, 1973*, Catalogue No. 68-207, Information Canada, Ottawa.

_____, *Provincial Government Finance, Revenue and Expenditure, 1972*, Catalogue No. 68-207, Information Canada, Ottawa.

_____, *Provincial Government Finance, Revenue and Expenditure, 1971.* Catalogue No. 68-207, Information Canada, Ottawa.

_____, *Provincial Government Finance, Revenue and Expenditure, 1969*, Catalogue No. 68-207, Information Canada, Ottawa.

_____, *Provincial Government Finance, Revenue and Expenditure, 1968*, Catalogue No. 68-207, Information Canada, Ottawa.

_____, *Provincial Government Finance, Revenue and Expenditure, 1961*, Catalogue No. 68-207, Information Canada, Ottawa.**

_____, *Provincial Government Finance, Revenue and Expenditure, 1960*, Catalogue No. 68-207, Information Canada, Ottawa.**

_____, *Federal Government Finance, Revenue and Expenditure, Assets and Liabilities, 1979*, Catalogue No. 68-211, Supply and Services Canada, Ottawa.

_____, *Federal Government Finance, Revenue and Expenditure, Assets and Liabilities, 1978*, Catalogue No. 68-211, Supply and Services Canada, Ottawa.

_____, *Federal Government Finance, Revenue and Expenditure, Assets and Liabilities, 1977*, Catalogue No. 68-211, Supply and Services Canada, Ottawa.

_____, *Federal Government Finance, Revenue and Expenditure, Assets and Liabilities, 1976*, Catalogue No. 68-211, Supply and Services Canada, Ottawa.

_____, *Federal Government Finance, Revenue and Expenditure, Assets and Liabilities, 1975*, Catalogue No. 68-211, Information Canada, Ottawa.

_____, *Federal Government Finance, Revenue and Expenditure, Assets and Liabilities, 1974*, Catalogue No. 68-211, Information Canada, Ottawa.

_____, *Federal Government Finance, Revenue and Expenditure, Assets and Liabilities, 1973*, Catalogue No. 68-211, Information Canada, Ottawa.

_____, *Federal Government Finance, Revenue and Expenditure, Assets and Liabilities, 1972*, Catalogue No. 68-211, Information Canada, Ottawa.

_____, *Federal Government Finance, Revenue and Expenditure, Assets and Liabilities, 1971*, Catalogue No. 68-211, Information Canada, Ottawa.

_____, *Federal Government Finance, Revenue and Expenditure, Assets and Liabilities, 1969*, Catalogue No. 68-211, Information Canada, Ottawa.

_____, *Federal Government Finance, Revenue and Expenditure, Assets and Liabilities, 1968,* Catalogue No. 68-211, Information Canada, Ottawa.

_____, *Financial Statistics of the Government of Canada, 1961,* Catalogue No. 68-211, Information Canada, Ottawa.**

_____, *Financial Statistics of the Government of Canada, 1960,* Catalogue No. 68-211, Information Canada, Ottawa.**

_____, *Estimates of Labour Income, Quarterly, 1978,* Catalogue No. 72-005, Supply and Services Canada, Ottawa.

Statistiques fiscales des particuliers du Québec, Analyse des déclarations des revenus des contribuables de la Province de Québec pour l'année 1977 et 1978, Gouvernement du Québec, Ministère du Revenu.

*"Taxation Statistics" was published by the Department of National Revenue, Taxation Division, now Revenue Canada.

**This publication was published by the Dominion Bureau of Statistics, the former name of Statistics Canada.